Spokane
A City For Living

Rick & Susie Graetz

by Michael Schmeltzer
Photos by Rick & Susie Graetz
Alan Bisson • Larry Mayer • The Spokesman-Review

American & World Geographic Publishing
and
New Media Ventures, Inc.

RICK & SUSIE GRAETZ PHOTOS

Above: "The Castle," where a modern-day princess or two may live, is now apartments.

Right: There is a park within a fifteen-minute walk of every neighborhood.

Title page: Riverfront Park's paths attract thousands of people daily in the summer.

Front cover: A legacy of Expo '74, Riverfront Park is one of Spokane's many treasures. ALAN BISSON

Back cover: Older established neighborhoods have a safe, welcoming feeling.
RICK & SUSIE GRAETZ

Library of Congress Cataloging-in-Publication Data
Schmeltzer, Michael.
  Spokane : a city for living / by Michael Schmeltzer.
    p. cm.
    Includes index.
    ISBN 1-56037-105-6
    1. Spokane (Wash.)--Guidebooks. 2. Spokane (Wash.)--Geography.
3 Spokane (Wash.)--Civilization. I. Title.
f899.S7s34 1996
979.7--dc20   96-31221
                                            CIP

Text © 1996 Michael Schmeltzer

© 1996 American & World Geographic Publishing and New Media Ventures, Inc.

This book may not be reproduced in whole or in part by any means (with the exception of short quotes for the purpose of review) without the permission of the publisher.

Write for our catalog:
American & World Geographic Publishing,
P.O. Box 5630, Helena, MT 59604.

A quiet elegance at sunset.

ALAN BISSON

Contents

A City for Living	7
The River	37
A Comfortable Home	45
Parks for the People	59
Kirtland Cutter	65
A Place to Learn and Work	69
From Fort Wright to Fairchild	76
Education International-Style	81
A Place to Play	85
Bloomsday	95

Above: The Monroe Street Bridge gracefully spans the Spokane River and is a vantage point for viewing the falls.

Top: Flowers for mom.

A City for Living

Spokane just might be the place that proves all those experts wrong. Who said today's cities have to be dirty, distressed and dangerous? Who said small cities can't make big things happen? Who said culture can't thrive far from a megalopolis? In Spokane, people are demonstrating that caring, vision, a little luck and lots of plain hard work can create an eminently livable community.

Downtown Spokane is clean, safe and healthy, still the business and retail magnet for a far-flung region. Older, close-in neighborhoods are thriving, even as new suburbs sprout like springtime wildflowers around the city's edges. Spokane's economy is strong and growing more diversified, generating new opportunities. Cultural amenities are expanding in scale beyond what one might expect of a city Spokane's size.

This is a city that is working, and working well. Spokane is robust, growing and gaining national renown as a place where good people still live the good life. In the mid-1990s, *Newsweek* declared Spokane a "Pacific Northwest paradise" and *Outside* magazine profiled Spokane and a few other small cities in a cover story titled "Dream Towns—Where to Find It All: A Real Job, A Real Life and the Big Outdoors."

Through the years, Spokane has assembled the elements essential to making the wheels of commerce turn. An early railroad hub, it remains a major regional transportation center. Hydroelectric power is abundant and inexpensive. It has modern communication systems, solid infrastructure, an excellent school system, a motivated and well-educated workforce. It has good police and fire departments, six major hospitals,

Above: The annual Tour des Lacs is a fun event for a good cause.

Facing page: Resembling a 16th century French chateau, the Spokane County Courthouse wears a golden wreath of leaves.

six colleges and universities. And aesthetics have not been ignored. Spokane has an expansive and well cared for public park system, a 2,700-seat Opera House and a new 12,500-seat multipurpose arena. The privately owned Metropolitan Performing Arts Center, a 750-seat venue affectionately known to locals simply as The Met, is an intimate, elegantly restored vaudeville-era theater that is a favorite of local audiences and artists ranging from the homegrown Uptown Opera company to Seattle grunge rockers Pearl Jam. Spokane is perhaps the smallest city in the country to support both a professional symphony orchestra, which celebrated its 50th season in 1996, and a professional theater company, which marked its 15th season that same year.

RICK & SUSIE GRAETZ

Looking peaceful and tranquil, the Spokane River flows through Spokane from Lake Coeur d'Alene.

Spokane is a center of commerce, culture, communications, transportation, medicine and education. It is the largest gathering of people in a largely unpopulated region of the country. Still, Spokane is relatively small. A recent count found 189,000 people living within Spokane's city limits and a total of 401,000 in Spokane County. The city sits at the edge of the Columbia Basin, where foothills of the Rocky Mountains rise toward the east. From here, it's a long day's drive to another city of real size: 290 miles to Seattle, 350 to Portland, 400 to Boise, and 480 to Calgary. This geographic isolation has enabled Spokane to grow up on its own, outside the shadow of a megalopolis, free to develop a unique identity and character. It has avoided the fate of many cities of similar size, such as Tacoma, forever overshadowed by its more glamorous big sister, Seattle.

As capital of its own domain, Spokane exerts influence considerably beyond what one would expect from a city of its size. Spokane is only the ninety-fourth largest city in the nation. But its region of influence takes in Eastern Washington, the northeast

Rick & Susie Graetz Photos

Left: Birdwatching in Liberty Park's natural area.

Below: A quality education is part of the Spokane lifestyle and Spokane Falls Community College makes it happen.

Bottom: Natural landscaping blends with the surroundings.

corner of Oregon, North Idaho, Western Montana, and even a portion of Canada. More than 1.7 million people live within this area. Most of these folks view Spokane as the big city—and as their big city. From throughout the region, they come to Spokane to do business, to seek medical treatment, to shop, or just to play golf or take in a touring Broadway show and enjoy dinner in one of the city's fine restaurants. "When my wife and I want to get away and enjoy a taste of the city for a day or two, we head down to Spokane," said Gerald Rotering, the former mayor of Nelson, British Columbia, about 150 miles north of Spokane. "To a lot of people who live around here, Spokane is much more our city than either Vancouver or Calgary."

Indeed, the Canada connection is strong in Spokane. Visitors from other parts of the country are sometimes surprised to find that Canada's flag flies alongside Old Glory almost everywhere in Spokane and that here the downtown parking meters accept both Canadian and American coins. Hockey games at the new Spokane Arena open with both national anthems. Spokane's five television stations, carried on cable throughout southeastern British Columbia and in Calgary and Edmonton, Alberta, have almost as many viewers in Canada as in the U.S. Many years, Spokane's public TV station, KSPS, gets the majority of its financial support from viewers north of the border.

RICK & SUSIE GRAETZ

A winter wonderland.

Many visitors come to Spokane to enjoy an encounter with the arts. Music and theater are staples of the city's cultural scene; both are hugely popular and well-patronized. Jack Lucas, general manager of G&B Select-A-Seat, the local box office outlet, said Spokane has supportive audiences for rock, jazz, folk and classical music, but that the big draw these days at new the 12,500-seat Spokane Arena is country. "Garth Brooks, Reba McEntire, George Strait, they'll sell out in a matter of hours," Lucas said. "Part of it is that country music has gotten to be big everywhere, but part of it is just the character of this area. Spokane was country long before country was cool." Another hot ticket is G&B's Best of Broadway series, which brings eight or ten touring Broadway shows to the Spokane Opera House every year. "The Best of Broadway series really helps set the tone for Spokane," Lucas said. "It's first-class, big-league entertainment. These are the same

COURTESY SPOKANE CHIEFS HOCKEY CLUB

Fans love the hard hitting, hard playing Spokane Chiefs.

shows that are playing San Francisco, Portland, Seattle, Denver." And Spokane can't seem to get enough, even of shows that have been this way before. In June 1996, "Les Miserables" made its third Spokane appearance in five years and again sold out all eight performances at the 2,700-seat Opera House.

The Opera House isn't the only place in Spokane to find live, professional theater. Spokane Interplayers Ensemble, the city's resident professional theater group, stages nearly 150 performances a year. Founded in 1981 by Bob and Joan Welch, Interplayers has built up a subscription base of more than 3,000 season ticket buyers. Add occasional show-goers and more than ninety percent of the tickets available during the season at Interplayers' 256-seat downtown showhouse will be sold. "That's phenomenal support for a city of this size," said Bob Welch. Spokane and New Haven, Connecticut, are the smallest cities in the country with successful, year-round professional theaters. "We've survived because people here don't just talk about supporting theater, they actually buy tickets." Interplayers produces seven plays per season, staging everything from

11

Rick & Susie Graetz Photos

Above: Smiling faces make visitors feel welcome.

Right: With six major hospitals, Spokane is one of the largest medical centers in the West.

Top: Skywalks connect more than fifteen blocks of downtown Spokane.

Shakespeare to Neil Simon. Spokane's theater audience is not only growing, but also growing more sophisticated. In most smaller cities, big-cast musicals are the only type of local production that can be counted on to put fannies into seats. "They have to depend on the friends and family of the cast to fill seats," Welch said. "Spokane audiences appreciate good theater for what it is. Even if they don't live next-door to the leading man or the kids in the chorus, they will come for the enjoyment of the art."

Like Interplayers, the Spokane Symphony Orchestra enjoys incredible community support. The orchestra, which plays forty-plus concerts a year, adds much to the richness of the city's social and cultural fabric. The Symphony brings to town several guest artists each year, ranging from jazz great Mel Torme to homegrown opera superstar Thomas Hampson. Its production of *The Nutcracker*, usually in conjunction with the Alberta Ballet, is a local Christmastime tradition. The orchestra's free summertime concerts in Spokane parks have gained fame not only for fine music but also for the audience's extravegent and elegant picnics.

Spokane nurseries burst with color in the spring.

The late sculptor Edward Kienholz liked to tell a story about growing up on a farm a few miles south of Spokane. "I would sit there on my stool milking cows, gazing out the barn door," Kienholz said. "Off above the hills to the northeast, I could see this great aura—the lights of Spokane glowing in the night sky —and I'd curse those damn cows and tell myself I was going to get the hell out of that smelly old barn. I wanted to see what those city lights were all about. I thought anything that bright had to be good." The artist's remembrance reveals something both about his own ambitions and about Spokane's appeal to many farm folks and small-town dwellers of the Inland Northwest. It's a mecca for many; a destination for the region's dreamers, its hopeful, its ambitious young.

Soon after graduating from high school, Kienholz made tracks for Spokane, where he attended college and worked before being lured away by the even brighter lights of Los Angeles. There he gained international stature in the 1960s for his powerfully satirical sculpture. Kienholz fused pieces of junk, architectural salvage, scrap metal and other cast-off objects into lifesize tableaus that are potent metaphors for modern American life. He returned to this area in the 1970s, and spent about half of each year

Feeding the ducks is a year-round attraction.

at a home-and-studio compound on Lake Pend Oreille, near Hope, Idaho, where he and his wife, Nancy Reddin Kienholz, continued to make art until he died of a heart attack in 1994. The artist's connection to Spokane was in some respects strong, in others quite tenuous. But the city appears, in ghostly form, in some of Kienholz's most important works. The artist salvaged sinks, tables, door frames, woodwork, chairs, beds and other odds and ends from old Spokane buildings that were demolished in the late 1970s and early 1980s and used them in a series of sculptures that many critics rank among his best. In these pieces, the artist used remnants of Spokane's past to tell in-your-face stories about the modern human condition. This series of sculptures was exhibited together in Spokane in 1984 before touring many of the country's major art museums. One piece, "Jesus Corner," now belongs to Spokane's Cheney Cowles Museum. After his death, a career retrospective of the artist's work opened at New York City's Whitney Museum of American Art, then moved to the Museum of Contemporary Art in Los Angeles, and then to the Berlinische Galerie in Germany. In his review of the Kienholz retrospective for *Time* magazine, art critic Robert Hughes wrote: "Kienholz wasn't a Pop artist....He was a history artist, working in a real-things-in-the-real-world vernacular...Compared with the thin, overconceptualized

Facing page: Sunlight warms a crisp winter day. LARRY MAYER

gruel that most political art in postmodern America has become...Kienholz was red meat all the way."

Given the lofty place to which native-son Ed Kienholz ascended in the world of contemporary art, it seems somewhat ironic that Spokane has not more enthusiastically embraced the visual arts. There is evidence of change, the most tangible being Gonzaga University's new 43,000-square-foot Jundt Art Center and Museum, which opened in 1995. "The Jundt is a huge step forward for the visual arts in Spokane," said Ralph Busch, of the city Arts Department. "It's a concrete symbol of the growing vitality of the arts overall, and of an increasing focus on the visual arts." Further evidence can be found in the growing public sculpture collection in Riverfront Park, which includes an eclectic group of works, highlighted by David Govedare's "The Joy of Running Together," a celebration in steel of Spokane's popular Bloomsday run; Ken Spiering's "Childhood Express," the giant red wagon loved by kids of all ages; Harold Balazs' "Centennial Sculpture," which appears to magically float in the Spokane River; and Deborah Copenhaver's contemplative bronze Vietnam memorial.

Riverfront Park is a reminder that back in 1974 Spokane sent out an invitation and the world came to visit. Ever since Expo 74, which drew 5.6 million people, the city has been doing its best to let people know the welcome mat is still out, and the effort is paying off in a steady stream of visitors. To some, that's no surprise. After all, Spokane offers an attractive mix of urban amenities and outdoor recreation opportunities.

RICK & SUSIE GRAETZ

Spokane homeowners show a great deal of pride in their property.

Still, the thing that many count as Spokane's single greatest asset is something that can't be had by tourists. "Day-to-day lifestyle is, to me, the best reason to be here," said Gary Beck, a 38-year-old computer consultant who grew up in Southern California and moved to Spokane in 1985. Beck and his wife, Lexie, a Montana native, recently considered a job offer that would have taken them back to California. After mulling it over for a few days, they decided to stay put. "I thought about the freeways and the smog and the outrageous real estate prices and the incredible crowds you run into anywhere

Dan McComb/The Spokesman-Review

Rick & Susie Graetz

Above: Sock it to 'em! From little folk to adults, soccer is a popular participation sport.

Right: Delicate beauty in a downtown alleyway.

A stroll through the park.

you go down there, and Spokane seemed pretty attractive," Beck said. "Here, the sky is blue instead of brown. You don't have to commute an hour each way to work. In the summer, I can leave my office at 5 o'clock, drive to Lake Coeur d'Alene and spend a couple of hours out on the boat and be back home before it's dark....I would have been making a lot more money, but what it came down to was that I honestly didn't think it would have bought as good a lifestyle as we have here."

C. Michael Archer, Spokane Area Chamber of Commerce communications director, has tracked relocation inquiries directed to the organization since 1989. Some months, the chamber receives several hundred calls and letters from people who want to know about Spokane. Some are taking job transfers here and just want to know what to expect once they arrive. Others are actively fishing for a place to live that's better than where they are now. "We get a lot of inquiries from people in California and the Puget Sound area—those places are one-two on the list—who want to know about the housing market and job opportunities, but who also have questions about quality-of-life issues: climate, crime rate, traffic, the public schools, recreation, cultural amenities."

Spokane has long been regarded as a slow-to-move, conservative city, a place that clings tightly to traditional values. It's probably a better place to be

COURTESY LIBBY PHOTOGRAPHERS/GONZAGA UNIVERSITY

An aerial view of Gonzaga University and the city.

Rick & Susie Graetz Photos

Above: A South Hill charmer.

Right: Ladies' day at Esmeralda Golf Course.

Top: The view from Cliff Drive looking toward Mount Spokane.

raising a family than to be single. Sue Weitz, a vice president at Gonzaga University, sees some truth in that. "I was single when I came here and I didn't find it to be a problem," said Weitz, who is now married with two children. "But we have had faculty members who felt that they just did not fit into Spokane as a single person. I think it's changing, but it's still frustrating for some people....One told me he just couldn't exist socially in this community." One Spokane native who now lives in Seattle describes his hometown as "Beaver Cleaverville—clean and wholesome, yes, but always two steps behind the times."

Others think that conservative label doesn't fit Spokane nearly as well as it once did. "It's not a cutting-edge kind of town, but it isn't as stodgy or red-neck as some people seem to think," said Frank Hoover, an attorney who grew up in New York and, after graduating from Gonzaga's law school, decided to go into practice in Spokane. "People here are open to new ideas, new attitudes."

Lazy days of summer.

Spokane, where 90-plus percent of the population is white, was one of the first cities in the West to elect a black mayor, James Chase. After Chase retired, the office was held in succession by two women, Vicki McNeill and Sheri Barnard. Spokane's innovative community policing program is touted as a national model. Spokane was also one of the first cities in the West to latch onto the idea of preserving its architectural heritage. While other cities went gung-ho after urban renewal—knocking down block after block of turn-of-the-century brick buildings to make way for modern glass-faced boxes—Spokane rehabilitated and renewed. There are new buildings, of course, but enough of the old remains to give Spokane the architectural face of a city that is stable, prosperous and aging gracefully. This led the National Trust for Historic Preservation to deem Spokane "one of the greatest architectural and preservation surprises in the West."

Indeed, downtown Spokane holds a treasure of historic buildings, a microcosm of the major architectural styles and building trends of early 20th century America. "One of the real strengths of downtown Spokane is its wonderful collection of well-preserved historic buildings," said John Abell, a professor of architecture and urban design at

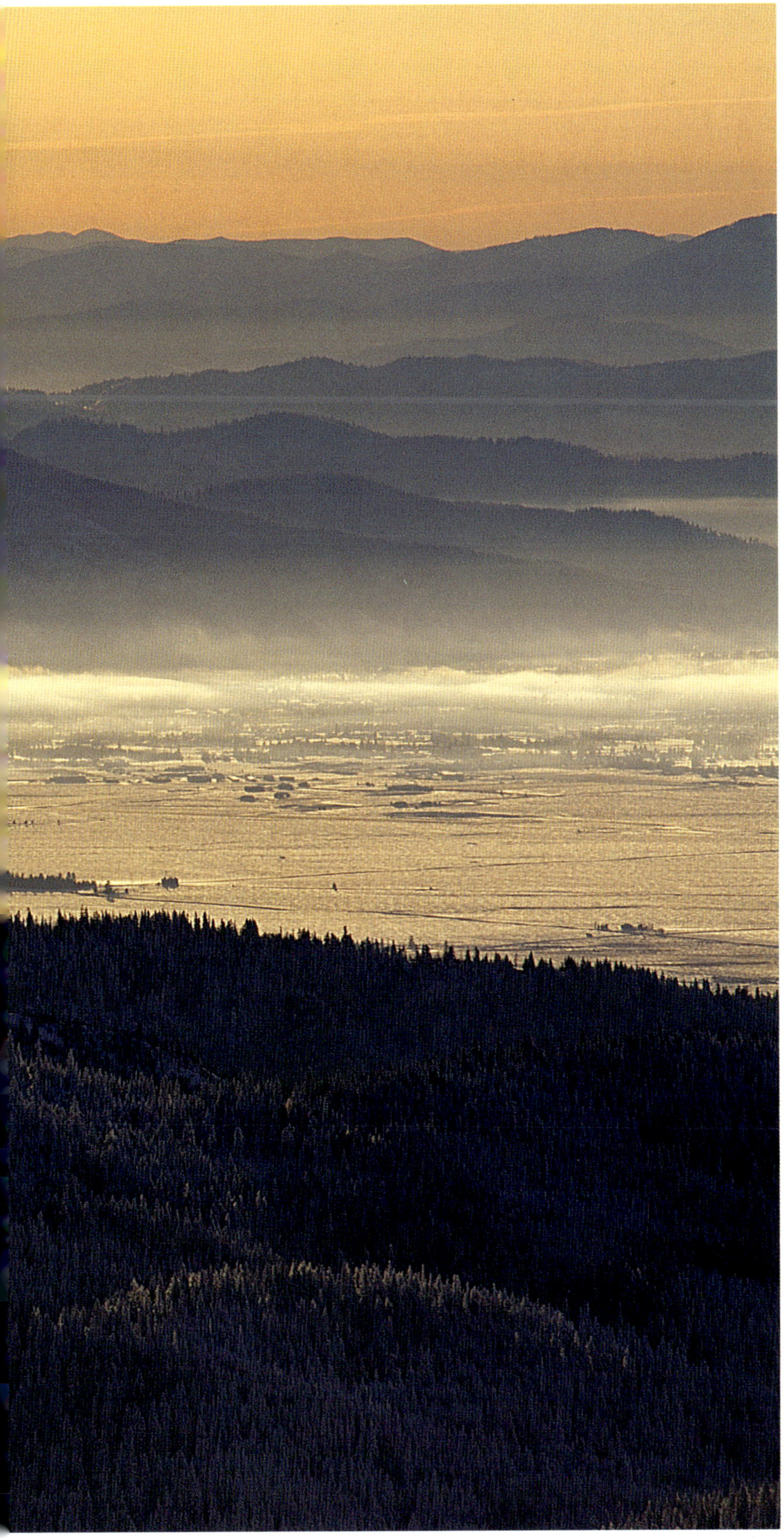

Rick & Susie Graetz

Rick & Susie Graetz

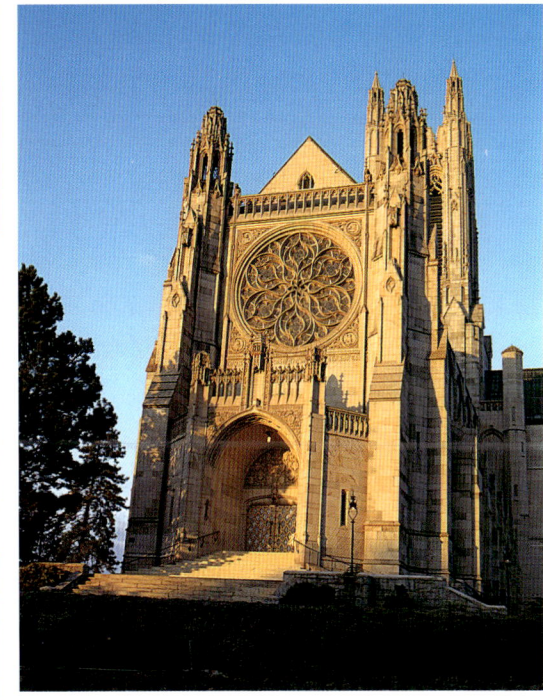

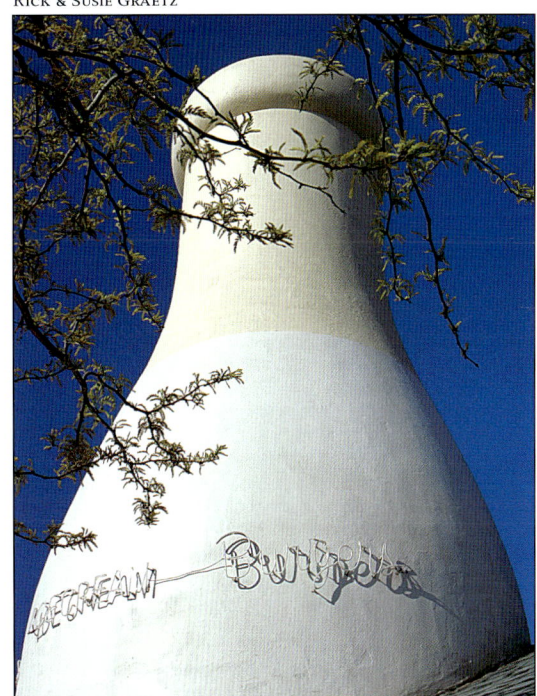

Above: In the Garland neighborhood, this milk-bottle–shaped cafe is the spot for treats.

Top: Carillon concerts ring from the Gothic spires of the Cathedral of Saint John the Evangelist.

Left: Misty mountains and cloud-covered valley east of Spokane.

Washington State University's Spokane campus. "These buildings give the downtown area a solid, people-friendly feel and a very human scale." In 1908, *The Western Architect*, then a leading design periodical, described Spokane as "the best built modern city of its size on the continent."

DAN McCOMB/THE SPOKESMAN-REVIEW

The right-of-way goes to the ducks on the Centennial Trail.

Take a stroll around downtown today and you'll encounter quite a number of handsome contemporary buildings, but you'll also find that many of the structures that so impressed the magazine's writers nearly a century ago are still vital threads in the city's urban fabric.

Start at the intersection of Riverside Avenue and Washington Street, where you'll find the U.S. Bank Building, still better known to many here as the ONB Building, for the original occupant, the locally owned Old National Bank. Designed by Chicago architect Daniel H. Burnham, this fifteen-story building, finished in cream-colored, glazed terra cotta, is a classic example of the early Chicago School skyscraper. Across Riverside is the Paulsen Center, actually two buildings that were erected in 1908 and 1928 by mining millionaire August Paulsen. The older, eleven-story brick structure at the east end of the block is a Florentine design. Local legend has it that when Paulsen saw that two business rivals had erected a six-story building down the street, he decided to put up an even taller building. Originally serviced by hydraulic elevators with quick-acting valves and lots of stretch in the wire rope, the elevator ride up and down the August Paulsen Building "was like no other, except in the amusements at Natatorium Park," recalled architectural historian R.B. Hyslop in his book, *Spokane Building Blocks*. The fifteen-story Paulsen Medical and Dental Building, designed by Spokane architect G.A. Pehrson, is exquisitely finished in

Left: A fast and rough stretch of the Spokane River flows through Riverside State Park.

Below: Pleasant Prairie rural school.

RICK & SUSIE GRAETZ PHOTOS

ALAN BISSON

The Gonzaga University crew gets an early morning workout on the Spokane River.

highly detailed polychrome glazed terra cotta. It is crowned by a penthouse apartment where trees grow on the terrace. A block to the south, at Sprague and Stevens, is the City Ramp Garage, a classic Art Deco design that originally employed a patented "pigeon-hole" parking system.

Heading west again on Riverside from Stevens, note the Gothic-inspired Sherwood Building along the north side of the street. Its extensive terra cotta detailing includes anatomically correct monkeys in gargoyle-style poses. Generally attributed to famed architect Kirtland Cutter, this 1916 building may actually have been designed by Pehrson, then a young associate in Cutter's office. Across the street, at Riverside and Howard, is the Rookery Building, another handsome Pehrson design in the Art Deco style.

At the southwest corner of Riverside and Lincoln is the Great Western Building, a six-story brick and brown terra cotta building that combines Beaux Arts and Chicago School design influences. When completed in 1900, it was said to have the fastest elevators in the West. This is the building that inspired August Paulsen's envy and efforts a few blocks to the east. Step inside to admire the gorgeous marble corridors and stairway and also note the "ESB" enscripted on doorknobs, door plates and elsewhere. Built by Charles Sweeney and F. Lewis Clark, two native New Yorkers, this was the original Empire State Building, predating the better-known Manhattan skyscraper by several years. At the west end of this block is the exclamatory Review Building, which

RICK & SUSIE GRAETZ

Pretty as a picture.

has commanded the intersection of Riverside and Monroe since 1891. Designed by architect Chauncey Seaton, this red-brick tower is one of the finest Romanesque revival buildings in the West. Along with the modern addition that stretches to the Great Western Building, it is occupied by *The Spokesman-Review* newspaper.

West of Monroe is the grand sweep of wonderfully eclectic yet exceptionally coherent architectural elements that make up the Riverside Avenue Historic District. On the south side of the street is the lovely Our Lady of Lourdes Cathedral, a twin-towered Romanesque revival monument built of red brick with sandstone trim. Its 1,200-seat sanctuary opened for Midnight Mass on Christmas Eve of 1903. Across the grassy, tree-lined park strip that bisects the curving avenue is a group of buildings that once made up Spokane's power row: The exclusive Spokane Club, a Cutter-designed Georgian revival completed in 1910; the Chamber of Commerce Building; the colonnaded Masonic Temple, designed by L.L. Rand; the former Elks Temple, an Italian renaissance design that has been adapted for use as headquarters for North Coast Life Insurance; the former funeral home that now houses offices.

Winter's blanket covers Spokane.

Downtown Spokane's most distinguished and best-known building is the Davenport Hotel, a fourteen-story structure that occupies a full city block at Sprague and Lincoln. Designed by Cutter for Louis Davenport, who started on the site in 1889 with a small waffle restaurant, the Davenport was once among the most elegant hotels in America. Guests included Queen Marie of Rumania, several presidents, movie stars, and other celebrities and dignitaries. The hotel shut down in the 1980s, and its reopening its viewed by many as a vital element in downtown's renaissance.

"Spokane takes a lot of pride in its past," said Penn Fix, a fourth-generation Spokane resident. "But it also looks to the future. I think that gives it a good balance." Fix left town after graduating from high school in the late 1960s. He returned ten years later, partly to become a partner in the family jewelry store, and partly because he found that he liked Spokane a whole lot better after spending a few years elsewhere. Fix said he has never regretted coming home. "The thing I like best about Spokane is that it's big enough that there's a lot going on, yet small enough that you can get involved," he said.

The name Spokane is taken from the Indian tribe that was living here long before the first white settlers arrived. A generally accepted translation of the word is "Children of the Sun" or "Sun People." Historically, the tribe was made up of three individual bands, all living along the river. The Middle Spokanes lived nearest to the site of today's city, occupying the lower reaches of the Latah Creek valley and the lowland benches just downstream from the falls. The Upper Spokanes inhabited an area to the east, in the general vicinity of present-day Post Falls, Idaho. The Lower band claimed the area below the confluence of the Spokane and Little Spokane rivers. The Spokanes are an Interior Salish people. They shared much culturally with such neighboring tribes as the Coeur d'Alenes, the Colvilles, the Kalispels and the Flatheads. Many other spots on area maps also take their names from Indian words: Okanogan (Salish for "meeting place") and Chewelah ("small, striped snake"), for example.

Equally common among place names and geographic labels in this area are French words: Coeur d'Alene ("heart of the awl"), Pend Oreille ("hanging ears") and Palouse ("grassland country"). That's because the first explorers to chart the Spokane country were the French Canadian trappers and traders of the Montreal-based Northwest Fur Company, led by explorer David Thompson. These Nor'Westers, as the Canadians called themselves, built a trading post on a piece of high ground at the confluence of the Spokane and Little Spokane rivers in 1810. Spokane House was the first place of business, and a profitable one, in what is now Washington state. When Thompson returned to eastern Canada in 1812, he took with him 9,000 beaver pelts from the Spokane district. The diaries of men who lived there portray the post as a place of pleasures,

LARRY MAYER

Lake Pend Oreille awaits spring and all of its activities.

too. Alexander Ross, who for a time was chief trader at Spokane House, wrote: "…There was a ball room, and no females in the land so fair to look upon as the nymphs of Spokane. No damsel could dance so gracefully as they; none were so attractive. But Spokane House was not celebrated for fine women only. There were fine horses, also. The race ground was admired, and the pleasures of the race. Altogether, Spokane House was a delightful place and time had confirmed its celebrity."

The Metropolitan Performing Arts Center, known as The Met, hosts a variety of attractions in grand style.

Ask people here today what they like about the area and sooner or later someone will mention the weather. Spokane is blessed with four distinct, pleasant seasons. The National Weather Service classifies ours as a "modified continental climate." It's basically a Rocky Mountain climate, moderated somewhat by Spokane's relative proximity to the Pacific coast. "There are an awful lot of people originally from Montana living in Spokane, and those folks feel right at home with the weather here," said Milton Maas, Spokane specialist for the National Weather Service. There are 200-plus sunny or mostly sunny days each year. Spokane averages just sixteen inches of rainfall annually, most of which falls during spring and late fall.

Spokane summers are sunny and warm, without the humidity in which many other parts of the country stew come July and August. The normal high temperature for a day in June is 74 degrees, for July 83 degrees, for August 82 degrees and for September 72 degrees. No Spokane summer would seem whole without a spell of hot weather. Usually, there are at least a couple of weeks with temperatures above 90 degrees, and two or three days when the thermometer at least flirts with the century mark. The hottest temperature ever recorded in Spokane is 108 degrees, a reading reached twice, on July 26, 1928, and on August 4, 1961. Even in the hottest stretches of summer, Spokane cools off nicely at night, temperatures typically dropping twenty to twenty-five degrees from the daytime high. Air conditioning is nice, but hardly a necessity of modern life.

In the spring, Spokane is drenched with colorful blossoms.

Spokane winters are snowy and cold, but not as bitter as in the Midwest's snow-belt cities. The normal low temperature for a day in November is 28 degrees, for December 21 degrees, for January 20 degrees, for February 25 degrees. The record cold is 31 degrees below zero, recorded on January 16, 1888. Spokane gets an average cumulative annual snowfall of fifty-one inches. Some years that snow seems to melt almost as soon as it falls; other years, it piles up and up. The winter of 1974-75 brought a total of 89 inches of snow, and eighty-seven inches fell in the winter of 1993-94, cheering skiers and snow-tire salesmen. But in Spokane the benchmark for snowy weather is the fabled winter of 1968-69. Total snowfall that year was just seventy-five inches, but so much of it was delivered by a rapid-fire series of January storms that on February 1 a record forty-two inches covered the ground. "That snow gets a little deeper every time someone tells a Californian about the winter of '69, but that's the record for snow depth: forty-two inches," said the National Weather Service's Maas.

The pleasant climate enables Spokane residents to fully enjoy the broad spectrum of outdoor recreation opportunities available practically in their own back yards. There are nineteen golf courses within forty-five minutes of the city, five downhill ski resorts within 100 miles, and seventy-six lakes within fifty miles of Spokane. The area presents nearby challenges for rock climbers, river rafters, runners, hikers and bikers, and others with a taste for outdoor fun.

A lot of folks here pursue another outdoor passion quite literally in their own back yard. For many in Spokane, gardening is more than just a hobby. It's an obsession. A survey conducted in 1991 for a national advertising association found that Spokane is

Right: This stately tower built in 1891 is home to The Spokesman-Review.

Below: Out and about on a crisp fall day.

RICK & SUSIE GRAETZ

DAN PELLE/THE SPOKESMAN-REVIEW

the country's number-one per capita market for all manner or garden goods, from shovels, hoses and seeds to greenhouse kits, beauty bark and plastic pink flamingos.

"I've always thought Spokane was a great gardening town in spite of its climate, rather than because of it," said Tonie Fitzgerald, a horticulturalist who heads up the popular Master Gardener program for Washington State University's cooperative extension office in Spokane. "Here, a nice garden doesn't just happen. You have to work hard at it. Things grow more slowly. Young plants can get frozen out. I've sometimes wondered if maybe the reason we're the country's number-one gardening market is because you have to keep buying and planting things over and over again."

Dance competitions and powwows celebrate the Native American culture that is closely tied to Spokane's beginnings.

Marilyn Smith, president of the Spokane Floral Association, admits that gardeners in Spokane face challenges, but said that's part of the fun. The floral association, one of twenty-one active communitywide gardening groups in Spokane, was founded in 1896 and today is the second-oldest garden club in the country, younger only than an organization in Athens, Georgia. It was a former Spokane Floral Association president, Ethyl Goodsell, whose love of a certain sweet-scented, blooming shrub gave Spokane its nickname, "Lilac City." Goodsell promoted the planting of lilac bushes in private yards and public parks. She also worked with leaders of other gardening groups to launch the city's Lilac Festival. The first Lilac Parade in 1938 consisted of a single float, from which schoolgirls threw sprigs of lilacs to onlookers, plus seven decorated automobiles. The Lilac Festival has grown into a springtime feel-good fixture in Spokane and the annual downtown parade now consists of more than fifty floats, dozens of marching bands, drill teams, equestrian units and other entries. "Lovely gardens are a Spokane legacy," Smith said. "There are beautifully tended yards in every neighborhood, not just in the fancier parts of town. People here take real pride in their homes, their neighborhoods, their community. I think beautifying our yards is one way we can all contribute, keep that legacy alive."

People who live in Spokane seem determined to do whatever they can to help make the city a better place. Volunteerism here is phenomenal. Jacque Ferrell-Fleury, director of the United Way of Spokane volunteer center, helps match people willing to donate their time and talents with some 250 local non-profit agencies looking for help. She estimates that the volunteers placed through the center contribute a combined twelve million hours a year to Spokane's neighborhood centers, schools, hospitals, the Salvation Army, Girl Scouts and many, many other worthwhile community causes. That's an average of about thirty hours per year for every man, woman and child in Spokane County—and, as Ferrell-Fleury points out, that estimate doesn't include time donated by volunteers whose help isn't recruited through United Way. "Spokane has a big, big heart," Ferrell-Fleury said. "We're way above the national norm in terms of volunteer community service. Many of our large employers—Washington Water Power, Hewlett-Packard, Boeing and others—really encourage their employees to get involved, and that helps set the tone. But people in Spokane just seem to believe in their community, and they believe in helping their community."

RICK & SUSIE GRAETZ

Winter doesn't slow Gonzaga's campus life down.

Today, Spokane is many things to many people. To some, the appeal is its intimate friendliness and old-fashioned values. To others, it's the easy access to urban amenities. Big town or small city, pick your pleasure. Here, you can find whichever you wish. Consider how two transplants, both now well-settled, longtime residents, view Spokane.

"What I like best about Spokane is that it's really just a big small town," said Judy Quinlivan, who came from Montana in the 1970s to attend Gonzaga University and decided to stick around. "You don't feel anonymous. It's friendly, safe, clean. It's a very comfortable, easy place to live."

Bob Welch, co-founder of Spokane Interplayers Ensemble, moved here from New York City in the 1950s. His take on Spokane is different, but no less real. "Spokane is a very charming little city," he said. "We have a professional symphony orchestra, professional theater, an up-and-coming opera company, and there's sculpture everywhere you look downtown....It's urban amenities, more than size, that make a city a city. I loved New York—I still do, as a place to visit. I love Spokane as a place to live."

Rick & Susie Graetz Photos

Above: This classic Japanese garden commemorates the good will, generosity and support of Spokane's sister city, Nishinomiya, Japan.

Right: Buildings in the Hillyard district are enlivened with historical murals.

35

Above: The Spokane River flows around Canada Island and through the center of Riverfront Park.
Facing page: An oasis in the middle of the city.

The River

It was the Spokane River that first lured people to the spot on which the city now stands, and perhaps as much as anything it is the river that has kept them here.

For the Spokane Indians, the river's salmon runs were a rich source of food. Settlers harnassed the river's power to run sawmills and flour mills and, once the mysteries of electricity had been solved by Thomas Edison and others, to light their streets, homes and offices. Today, the Spokane continues to brighten our homes and turn the wheels of commerce and industry. It offers residents myriad recreational opportunities. An integral element of the city's identity, the river serves both as a symbol of Spokane and a source of community pride. More than that, its power and beauty nurture the city's soul.

Franz Schneider, a poet and longtime professor at Gonzaga University, sees the river and its falls as a metaphor for life itself. "There is power, beauty, mystery, even danger there," he said. "And above it all, when the sun shines through the mist, you see the rainbow—the symbol of peace, harmony, promise....The river makes the city's heart beat."

Standing on Riverfront Park's footbridge, suspended across the river just above its thundering falls, one can appreciate both the river's awesome power and its magnificent beauty. The sight and sound are spectacular: foaming water thundering through a rocky gorge, the cold spray shimmering in the sunlight as it hangs 100 feet above. Few cities have been so blessed by nature. And few have shown their appreciation for such a blessing quite so well as Spokane.

The Spokane is a Class A waterway, a state designation that means it is clean enough to swim and fish. Trout spawn in places where the river, long ago tamed by seven hydroelectric dams, still runs swift. Deer and even an occasional moose munch the leafy brush that grows along the riverside. Osprey nest on old pilings and bald eagles and great blue herons fold their massive wings and rest in the tall trees by its banks.

"The Spokane, today, is a very healthy river," said Dr. Ray Soltero, an Eastern Washington University biologist who has studied the river since the 1970s. "I certainly wouldn't have a problem eating fish caught just about anywhere on the Spokane."

Soltero knows that has not always been the case. "For many years, the Spokane River functioned almost as an open sewer," Soltero said. The city dumped raw human and industrial wastes directly into the river. By 1909, the Spokane had become so polluted that the state health department issued a cease and desist order, forbidding the city to discharge sewage into the river. Apparently no one here paid much attention, because the state continued to issue such edicts almost annually for the better part of the next half-century. In 1938, a state health department list of problem waterways described the Spokane as "grossly polluted," as a "serious health hazard" and ranked the river as the foulest waterway in Washington. In the 1940s, the city attempted a crude cure, dumping tons of gravel into the river where the sewer pipes discharged; it was believed that the gravel would scrub and purify the sewage as it flowed into the river. The city didn't build its first real sewage treatment plant until 1958—and it would be more than a decade after that before a facility big enough to effectively handle Spokane's wastes was in place and functioning.

Wonder mixes with wariness at the Riverfront Park Petting Zoo.

Early morning fishing near Gonzaga University.

"It was a stinking mess," Soltero said. "But the city, along with the state Department of Ecology and the [federal] Environmental Protection Agency, has worked very hard to clean up the river. The effort has been aggressive and progressive....As a scientist, I think they've succeeded in restoring a pretty sick river to remarkably good health."

The Spokane River flows from the north end of Idaho's Lake Coeur d'Alene. It is fed by the melting snowpack in the Bitterroot mountain range, the crest of which divides Idaho and Montana. Mountain snowmelt runs into the St. Maries, the St. Joe and the Coeur d'Alene rivers, all of which find their way into Lake Coeur d'Alene. The lake's only outlet, the Spokane follows a winding, 111-mile course carved into the basalt plateau many thousands of years ago by glacial runoff, then pours itself into the great Columbia River. Along the way, it flows over seven dams and under more than seventy bridges. It sweeps past farms, factories, four college campuses, and an Indian reservation. It lends itself for view from mansions and luxury condominiums, and also from the porches of Peaceful Valley's humble cottages and the trailer homes in the San Sousi senior citizen park.

According to the mythology of the Spokane tribe, the riverbed was created by a giant dragon. The invading monster, after wreaking havoc on the countryside, had fallen asleep at the spot where the Spokane River empties into the Columbia. The Indians discovered the dragon there and, in Lilliputian fashion, tried to secure the sleeping beast by tying him to the nearby trees and rocks. Then, to avenge the destruction, they attempted to kill him. Their weapons, however, had only the effect of waking the dragon. Once roused from his sleep, the dragon stomped off toward the east, dragging the trees and boulders behind him, until he fell into Lake Coeur d'Alene. Just as the Spokanes' folklore explains how the channel that carries the water from Lake Coeur d'Alene to the Columbia River was carved, tribal mythology also tells how the great Spokane falls—where the river drops 150 feet over a half-mile stretch of roaring rapids and swirling plunges—came to be. In this story, the daughter of a Spokane chief marries a Spokane man named Moxnoose, but then loses her heart to an Okanogan man, Stinging Bee. The lovers meet on the hill south of the river and decide to poison Moxnoose. After doing so, they rendezvous at the river's edge—only to be confronted by the ghost of Moxnoose. The angry ghost turns Stinging Bee into a mass of rocks and hurls him into the river, creating the lower falls. The ghost then casts his unfaithful wife into the river beneath the falls so that she will forever bear the terrible pressure of the water pouring over Stinging Bee. The apparition then turned himself into a second mass of rocks upriver, from where he continues to watch the river punish those who betrayed him.

The Spokane River has a multitude of spirited personalities. In spring, swollen by mountain snowmelt, the Spokane is a raging torrent. In the dog days of a dry summer, the river slows to a comparative trickle and can appear almost thirsty. The Spokane's character changes in other ways along its 111-mile course. Early on, it's like a long, lazy

A quiet afternoon on the Spokane River east of the city.

Rick & Susie Graetz

Rick & Susie Graetz Photos

Right: Picnicking in the park.
Below: The Gondola Skyride gets up close and personal with the thundering Spokane Falls.

41

arm of Lake Coeur d'Alene. Even big boats can follow the river as far as Post Falls, site of the hydroelectric dam that since 1906 has regulated the lake level. Beyond Post Falls Dam and the state line, in the Sullivan Park area of the Spokane Valley, the river crashes through rapids wild enough to make a kayaker's heart pound. The Spokane's flow softens again and turns to slackwater as it nears Millwood, the town that grew up around the Inland Empire Paper Company mill. Along the riverbank near the mill is an experimental 110-acre plantation on which the paper company raises fast-growing poplar trees. The trees are irrigated with effluent from the mill, significantly reducing the volume discharged into the river. After only five years, the poplars are big enough to harvest for use as pulp.

Near Upriver Dam is the water pumping station where the city taps into the Spokane-Rathdrum Prairie Aquifer, the giant underground river that is the sole source of drinking water for the Spokane-Coeur d'Alene region. The aquifer flows through a deep layer of coarse gravel beneath the river, following its path roughly from Lake Coeur d'Alene to the falls downtown, then turning to the north while the river flows in a westerly direction. The river and the aquifer are interwoven, exchanging water in several places. Swimmers at Boulder Beach along Upriver Drive sometimes encounter surprisingly cold pockets of water in the river. This is simply a place where the water table is higher then the river bottom, allowing the colder aquifer and the river to mix together. The interchange between the flow of the river and the flow of the aquifer is one reason that maintaining the health of the river is so important. Polluting the river is a lot like peeing into your drinking water.

As it courses downstream toward the Columbia, the Spokane changes from fast-running river to reservoir slackwater and back again as it passes each dam. In places, such as where it boils and churns past the Bowl and Pitcher rock formation in Riverside State Park, the Spokane still appears untamed. Kayakers and rafters love this stretch of river for its wild, whitewater thrills.

Improvements in the river's water quality these past decades have gone hand-in-hand with efforts to beautify the riparian environment and make the river itself more accessible to the people of Spokane. Riverfront Park—a green jewel in the heart of downtown that as recently as the early 1970s was an ugly tangle of railyards that sealed the river off from the city—is a good example of how these efforts have succeeded. So is the Centennial Trail, which follows the river from Spokane all the way upriver to Lake Coeur d'Alene and downriver to the confluence of the Spokane and Little Spokane. The trail, begun in the 1980s, is hugely popular with walkers, joggers, bicyclists and others seeking exercise, fresh air and an opportunity to commune with nature.

Growth puts great pressure on the Spokane River. More people mean more houses, more cars, more industry, more waste. "We have to be cognizant of our role in relationship to the environment," said biologist Ray Soltero. "Almost everything associated with growth has the potential to affect the river. I'm not against growth, but as we plan

Spokane's riverbanks have a clean, colorful appearance.

for and make the decisions that guide growth, we must always think in terms of protecting this resource."

Indeed, the river is too precious to ignore. There are bigger, perhaps even more beautiful rivers in the world. But none makes the heart of a city pound quite like the thundering Spokane.

ALAN BISSON

Above: A walk on the wild side of the Centennial Trail.
Facing page: Singer Patrice Munsel's former home across from Cannon Hill Park.

A Comfortable Home

John Abell was excited about moving west from Washington, D.C., in the early 1990s. He was looking forward to a new job as professor of architecture and urban planning at Washington State University, and to the opportunity to help launch the university's new Spokane branch campus. He was eager to get out and enjoy the nearby mountains, the lakes and rivers. What Abell, a native of the northeastern United States, wasn't so sure about was how much he would actually enjoy living in a smaller, relatively isolated city like Spokane. Five years later, he's "happy as heck to be here."

The reasons are many. The job is going well, and the outdoor recreation is all that he had imagined. He's made friends, and gotten involved in community affairs, such as serving on the Spokane Arts Commission. But what does he like best about his new hometown? "My very favorite thing about Spokane," Abell said, "is the wonderful neighborhood that I live in."

Abell and his wife Nancy live in an older home on a quiet, tree-lined street near Manito Park on the city's South Hill. It's the kind of leafy, well-kept neighborhood that seems to throw open its arms and cry "Welcome home!" the first time you drive down the street.

The scene on a summer evening seems positively Rockwellian: Families sitting on front-porch swings, an elderly couple walking their terrier, kids on bicycles chasing the happy jingle of the ice cream truck.

What's most remarkable about this scene isn't that newcomers John and Nancy Abell

RICK & SUSIE GRAETZ PHOTOS

Right: A familiar corner in the Liberty Park neighborhood.

Below: Many of Hillyard's wonderful old buildings now house interesting antique shops.

46

A stately Sumner Avenue home.

found it near Manito Park, but that it's played out, with subtle variations, all over town. Spokane is a community of diverse and truly delightful neighborhoods, from the genteel South Hill to striving, blue-collar Hillyard to ultra-urban Carnegie Square to the horsey suburbs of the Spokane Valley. Most people who live here like where they live. They're proud of their homes, they're comfortable in their neighborhoods, and they have a very real sense of connection to their community.

"One of the salient things about Spokane is the way people care about and identify with their neighborhoods," Abell said. "I think that's one of the reasons the city's older neighborhoods—on the South Hill, West Central, the Garland area—are still so vital. They haven't been abandoned. They've always been inhabited by people who genuinely appreciate and care about them."

Abell said he and his wife were drawn to their Craftsman-style bungalow by the warm charm of the house itself, but even more so by its surroundings. "We loved the park and we still use it every day," he said. "We liked our house, of course, but we also were attracted by the character of the other homes in the area, the scale of the neighborhood. I liked that there's a small commercial area within walking distance, where we could go to pick up a video, or get some ice cream or a cup of coffee. But the other thing I've discovered since we've been here is that this beautiful neighborhood environment has attracted other people who appreciate it, just like Nancy and I do. Right there you have something in common with your neighbors. That shared interest in and affection for the neighborhood facilitates a social structure; it creates a bond."

The South Hill is the oldest of Spokane's prestige addresses. Grand mansions built by timber barons, mining millionaires and merchant princes line Sumner Avenue in the Cliff Park neighborhood, a district listed on the National Register of Historic Places because of its architectural significance. These homes designed in the Mediterranean, Tudor, French chateau, arts and crafts, shingle, Jacobethan, Georgian revival and California mission styles were the work of some of the best architects practicing in the Northwest in the early 20th century. Replace the pines growing here with palm trees and this could be a streetscape straight out of Beverly Hills.

Spokane's sidewalks invite folks out for a walk.

But certainly not every home on the South Hill is a well-aged architectural masterpiece. The vast majority of houses here were not built for and are not occupied by the rich, but rather by middle-class folks. That's true of the Cliff Park district, too, Sumner Avenue notwithstanding. On nearby Cotta and Sound avenues and Wall and Stevens streets, the houses and the lots upon which they sit are smaller than the Sumner Avenue estates, but most are of the same well-seasoned vintage, and many have an abundance of the sort of architectural niceties—columns, stucco and half-timber detailing, elaborate brick and stone work outside; inglenook fireplaces and fancy hardwood trim inside—that led local real estate agents to coin the well-worn descriptive phrase "South Hill charmer."

Similarly charming older neighborhoods can be found all over the lower South Hill and on Spokane's near North Side, as well.

Such city neighborhoods benefited greatly from the early Spokane passion for building parks. In 1908, when the Spokane Park Board commissioned the country's leading landscape architects, Olmsted Brothers of Brookline, Massachusetts, to draw up a master plan for development of a public park system, Park Board president Aubrey L. White also asked the firm to outline a general design for the young city itself. Spokane had grown up in grid fashion. The Olmsteds saw an opportunity for something more

Left: A cozy house and yard.

Below: This tree-lined boulevard lends a park-like atmosphere to the neighborhood.

RICK & SUSIE GRAETZ PHOTOS

artistic. They proposed diagonal boulevards, both as a means of moving traffic more efficiently and of creating aesthetic variety. The designers suggested that streets through residential neighborhoods should follow the terrain, curving around natural features such as rock outcroppings, which would be left intact rather than blasted out, and that even in relatively flat, open areas neighborhood streets be allowed to meander a little. And they proposed planting ornamental trees along virtually all city streets.

Many of the day's real estate developers took note. The South Hill particularly has a number of neighborhoods that appear to have been laid out following the Olmsted guide. The Cannon Hill, Cliff Park, and Rockwood districts, built up shortly after the Olmsted report was written, are all departures from the grid system. Spring-fed ponds, rugged basalt bluffs and other dramatic natural features were left intact, and the shape of many building lots also departed from the traditional rectangle. The far west end of the West Central neighborhood also was developed at about that same time and exhibits some design similarities: gracefully curving streets, irregularly shaped building lots, plenty of street trees. Today, Spokane's citywide urban forest includes about 100,000 leafy trees growing streetside in the public right-of-way. These Norway maples, black locusts, sycamores, elms, oaks and other trees, planted in the early decades of the 20th century, are now giants, creating glorious green canopies overhanging neighborhood streets in summer, a blaze of brilliant gold, red and rust in autumn.

Close calls and fast action are the norm at Spokane Indians games.

Neighborhood traditions help neighbors connect with one another, fostering a greater sense of community and belonging. Residents of the Cliff Park district gather three or four times a year for neighborhood potlucks. At Easter, neighborhood children hunt for colored eggs and candy hidden in the park. And it is not just the parents of preschoolers who help make the egg hunt happen. Older neighbors whose children are grown and gone often dye a dozen or two just for the fun of seeing the wonder and delight on a the face of a five-year-old who has been visited by the Easter bunny. On the Fourth of July, there's a neighborhood parade.

Colin Mulvany/The Spokesman-Review

Rick & Susie Graetz

Above: A solid neighborhood sentry.

Right: Planting annuals in the formal European-style Duncan Garden.

Top: Polished to perfection.

Rick & Susie Graetz

Peace and tranquility in the Nishinomiya Japanese Garden.

Traditions are alive and well elsewhere, too. The Hillyard Festival, which combines a parade, a carnival, a food fair, a classic car show, a street dance and a sidewalk sale into one weekend-long celebration, has been an annual summertime event in that northeast Spokane neighborhood for years. "It really brings people together, gives us a chance to have some fun, to reminisce," said Bob Apple, owner of the Comet Tavern on Market Street, Hillyard's main drag.

In Hillyard, reminiscences almost always involve railroading. Originally a separate city, Hillyard was annexed to Spokane by a vote of its residents in 1924. The name honors Great Northern Railway founder James J. Hill, who built a locomotive manufacturing facility here as part of his huge regional rail maintenance and switching yard—hence, Hill's yard became Hillyard. The Great Northern once employed 6,000 people here, but Hillyard operations shut down in the mid-1970s, just a few years after the big railroad merger that created Burlington Northern. Once a thriving collection of small businesses—bakeries, banks, cafes, hardware stores, even a Studebaker dealership—Hillyard's Market Street commercial district hit the skids after the railroad pulled out.

But now, by looking to the past, Hillyard is creating a bright future for itself. Many of the Market Street storefronts today house newly thriving shops selling antiques and collectibles. A cafe, a florist shop, a stamp shop and other small neighborhood businesses have opened, and business and property owners have organized an association to promote the district. The business association has begun an ambitious mural program that helps to improve the appearance of the area and also honors Hillyard's history. Two large railroad-themed murals were painted on the sides of buildings in 1994 and 1995 by artist Tom Quinn, one at Market and Wellesley, the other at Market and Olympic. A third, by artist Rolf Goetzinger, was done in 1996, also at Market and Olympic. Larry Thomas, who owns Hillyard Florist and is chairman of the mural committee, hopes to commission one new painting each year "until we have a mural on the side of every possible building."

Railroad engineer Frank Kerr has lived in Hillyard all his life. His father, a Great Northern engineer from 1917 until 1962, helped him get a job with the railroad right after Frank graduated from Rogers High School in 1956. Likewise, Frank helped his son, Dan, get on with Burlington Northern after he graduated from Rogers in 1975. The murals and other improvements to the Hillyard business district are promoting neighborhood pride, according to Frank Kerr. "They're on the right track," he said of the effort to move the neighborhood forward while also celebrating its past. "I know a lot of old railroaders who retired and stayed right in the neighborhood. They're real proud of those murals."

Another North Side neighborhood that has seen something of a renaissance in recent years is the Garland district. Here, nice, older homes surround a lively, pedestrian-friendly commercial area with two local landmarks as architectural bookends: the vintage Garland Theater, a classic 1940s movie house, and a building shaped like a giant milk bottle that houses a cafe. In between are two blocks of shops: a book store, a music shop, a bakery, a camera-repair shop, another cafe, a couple of taverns, and more. "It's the type of neighborhood that pushes the nostalgia buttons in a lot of people," said Mike Adolfae, director of the city's Community Development Department. "It's a place

RICK & SUSIE GRAETZ

Roy Shioski, longtime owner and operator of the Hillyard Cleaners and Laundry.

where a kid in the neighborhood can hop on his bike and ride down to the Milk Bottle for an ice cream, or to the Garland for the $1 matinee." It's also the only Spokane neighborhood to "graduate" from the city's Community Development program, which funnels federal money into low-income areas for revitalization projects ranging from street paving to home rehabilitation. New people moving into the neighborhood raised the income level to the point that it no longer qualified for federal help.

Students enjoy a spacious campus at Spokane Community College.

The successful gentrification of Carnegie Square just west of downtown has brought an exciting mix of residential, commercial and professional office uses into an area that once was a seedy stretch of Spokane's Skid Road. Integrus Architecture jump-started the neighborhood's heart in 1992 when it acquired the long-vacant but still lovely former Carnegie Library on Cedar Street between First and Sprague avenues and renovated the building for its offices. Architect-developer Ron Wells and his wife, Julie, an interior designer, meanwhile acquired and rehabilitated four other buildings clustered around the intersection of First and Cedar: the old Eldridge Buick building, which once housed Spokane's biggest automotive showroom, two turn-of-the-century apartment buildings fronting on the Cedar Street park strip, and an old hotel. Today, Carnegie Square is home to a couple of hundred mostly young apartment dwellers, art and antique galleries, a wine shop, a restaurant and bagel bakery, a coffee roaster, a bicycle shop, a hair salon, and a number of professional offices. "It's a classic urban neighborhood reborn," said John Abell of WSU's School of Architecture. According to the state historic preservation office, it's also a classic success story. In 1996, Carnegie Square's developers received an award for their renovation and restoration work.

In many of the Spokane area's newer suburban neighborhoods, the appeal is country-style living, with the emphasis on getting close to nature. How close? In the spring of 1996, a grizzly bear wandered through a subdivision of ten-acre Deer Park area ranchettes. It was the first confirmed sighting of a grizzly in Spokane County in more than 100 years. In the Spokane Valley, the animal of interest in subdivisions featuring small acreages is usually the horse. Today, much of the Valley is urban in both density and character. But Otis Orchards, Greenacres, and most of the far southern reaches of the Valley remain rural in nature, and the land is zoned for growing crops and raising

RICK & SUSIE GRAETZ PHOTOS

Left: Spokane has a national reputation for medical innovation and quality patient care. Deaconess and Sacred Heart are well-known for their neonatal intensive care and trauma treatment facilities.

Below: Fresh produce, ethnic foods and local crafts abound at the summer Market Place.

Right: Built in the 1940s, the Garland Theater is part of the charm of the Garland district.

Below: A great many Spokane homes use natural rock formations as part of the landscape.

RICK & SUSIE GRAETZ PHOTOS

Salesman extraordinaire.

farm animals. While there aren't many commercially viable farm or ranch operations here any more, there are a lot of "hobby farmers" with five- or ten-acre tracts, where they graze a few horses and grow a little hay.

Holly Gallinger and her family built a home in a Greenacres subdivision called Saltese Estates in 1984. The house sits on ten acres of pine trees and meadows naturally irrigated by a small creek and has a lovely view of Mica Peak. The family has two horses and ten-year-old daughter Megan is involved in 4-H and takes riding lessons. "I love the setting—the view, the wildlife, all of it," Holly Gallinger said. "But what I love most is the privacy and the peace and quiet. I like having neighbors, but I like having a little elbow room, too. Our neighbors are very friendly and they're great about helping when the need arises. But they're also real good about leaving each other alone. You see each other when you want to because you want to, not because you neighbor is right there every time you step out the back door."

City or country, north or south, Spokane's neighborhoods share one thing: residents who truly care, about their neighbors and their neighborhoods. "I know people on the South Hill think that's the place to live in Spokane," said railroader and lifetime Hillyard resident Frank Kerr. "People in Hillyard watch out for each other, they take care of each other. I've honestly never wanted to live anywhere else."

Alan Bisson

Rick & Susie Graetz

Above: Free symphony concerts like this one in Comstock Park are social highlights of the summer.

Right: Functional art means fun for youngsters playing on Ken Spiering's sculpture titled "Childhood Express."

Facing page: Antique, hand-carved, painted ponies dance to old-time organ music in Riverfront Park.

58

Parks for the People

The pioneers who built Spokane took considerable pride in their creation. They were interested in economics, of course, but also in aesthetics. Spokane, they were determined, would be more than a good place to make a living. It would also be a good place to live. Today, that determination lives on—and nothing illustrates it quite so beautifully as Spokane's public parks system.

Today there is a park within a ten- or fifteen-minute walk from virtually every home in the city. There are small, quiet parks like five-acre Cliff, a mostly natural patch of pine-studded green surrounding a distinctive basalt butte, the top of which yields lovely city views. There are active parks, like eight-acre A.M. Cannon, where West Central neighbors can swim, swing, slide, picnic, play basketball, or tennis. There are big, showplace parks like ninety-acre Manito, with its elegant formal gardens, and 100-acre Riverfront, built around the roaring river falls in the heart of downtown. There are four municipal golf courses, six swimming pools, seven community centers, two large sports complexes for adults and two more for children, an art center housed in a historic mansion, fourteen separate parcels of conservation land, and a sixty-five-acre arboretum with a meandering little creek and a big collection of native and cultivated trees and plants.

Altogether, the Spokane Parks Department owns 3,500 acres of protected green space—parks, playfields, pathways and nature preserves, free for all to enjoy. By comparison, Tacoma has 1,600 acres of park lands, Wichita has 1,200 acres, Salt Lake City has

Rick & Susie Graetz Photos

Above: Coeur d'Alene Park, the first public park in Spokane.

Right: Seventy-five years young and a true Lilac City fan.

1,000. Per capita, Spokane has one of the most expansive municipal parks systems in the country.

"What's amazing to me is that the city had already acquired about three fourths of that land before World War I," said Judy Quinlivan, Parks Department recreation manager. "Early on, Spokane was a national leader in the development of a citywide park system....People here have always been really proud of our parks, and rightfully so. Parks are a vital and wonderful part of Spokane's identity."

Much thanks for that goes to early day city beautification advocate Aubrey L. White and other early civic leaders who had the good fortune of getting excellent advice and the good sense to follow it.

In 1908, the Spokane Park Board hired the nation's leading landscape architecture firm, Olmsted Brothers of Brookline, Massachusetts, to draw up a plan for a citywide parks system. The Olmsteds noted that Spokane had "remarkable opportunities for preserving big and strikingly picturesque landscape features for its parks." The city, which owned just 173 acres of park land, was told that it should aim to acquire 2,500 acres for parks. To create real urban beauty, the Olmsteds said, Spokane should not only develop landscaped parks and playfields, but also build treed greenbelts into its streets and parkway drives along the river. The Olmsteds also recommended that some of Spokane's "strikingly picturesque" park land be preserved more or less in its natural state.

White, who had earned a modest personal fortune shortly after the turn of the century selling stocks to Eastern investors, was Spokane's first Park Board president. It was he who had urged the city to hire the Olmsteds, and he who ensured that the Olmsted plan would be carried out. White counted among his personal friends many, if not most, of early day Spokane's business elite: real estate investors F. Lewis Clark and William J.C. Wakefield, mining man John Finch, hotel owner Louis Davenport, bankers Joel E. Ferris and Robert L. Rutter, and newspaper publisher William H. Cowles, among others. White referred to these men as "my powerhouse." He asked for and received their help during the successful 1910 campaign for a $1 million park bond,

ALAN BISSON

Picnics, potlucks and pig out in the parks.

Teaching her babies to swim in Manito Park.

then turned to them again and again in coming years for help in building Spokane's park system.

From 173 acres in 1908, the park system grew to 1,933 acres by 1915. The city had acquired that land at a cost of $729,000, while Seattle, another Olmsted client, had spent $2.5 million during roughly the same period to buy 1,803 acres for parks. Spokane was able to spend so much less than Seattle while systematically acquiring even more park land in large part because White was able to convince his "powerhouse" friends and others to either buy or donate desirable land for parks. Many of Spokane's best-loved parks—Audubon, Cannon Hill, Cliff, Corbin, Coeur d'Alene, Hays, Liberty, Manito and others—were gifts to the city from early citizens.

Among Spokane's city parks, none is more lovely or varied than Manito. This South Hill gem contains 90 acres of formal gardens, a conservatory, a large pond that is home to ducks and swans, scenic drives, peaceful natural areas, tennis courts and picnic and play areas. Duncan Garden, a classical European renaissance-style garden that includes three acres of manicured lawns and colorful bedding plants, and the tranquil Nishinomiya Japanese Garden are favorite places for outdoor summertime weddings. More than 1,500 rose bushes, both old-fashioned and modern varieties, bloom on Manito's Rose Hill. The Gaiser Conservatory, with three large public rooms filled with colorful and fragrant tropical plant specimens, is a lush haven on a cold, gray winter day.

During summer, a small cafe inside the park serves light fare alfresco to diners who sometimes share their lunch with friendly squirrels.

Given the historic nature of Spokane's system, it's a little ironic that one of the city's newest parks has become perhaps its most widely known and best-loved. One-hundred-acre Riverfront, which straddles the Spokane River on the former world's fair site, is the crowning jewel of the park system. With broad rolling lawns, flower beds, shade trees, paths for strollers, skaters and bicyclists, and, of course, the cool river, it attracts thousands of people daily during summer. Downtown office workers come to stretch their legs, to eat a sack lunch, or just to relax in this middle-of-the-city oasis. The Clocktower, all that remains of the Great Northern Railway's Spokane station, is a reminder that not so long ago this lovely park was a blighted inner-city railyard. Across the river is another icon of Spokane's past: the historic Looff Carousel, still spinning merrily around. The Riverfront Park Pavilion housed the popular United States Pavilion during Expo 74. Today, it's still an entertaining place, with a skating rink, miniature golf, a handful of amusement rides, and the Imax Theater, which boasts a screen five stories tall.

The value of Spokane's parks to the city's residents is impossible to compute. They offer recreation and relaxation. They add natural beauty to our urban setting. Certainly, Spokane is a better place to live because of its wealth of park lands.

"We're forever indebted to the community's early leaders," said Ron Sims, a Spokane architect and former president of the city Park Board. "We wouldn't have the park system we have today—which in my mind is one of Spokane's greatest assets—without them."

A discerning gardener.

RICK & SUSIE GRAETZ

Continuing the tradition established early on by Aubrey L. White and others is the Park Board's mission today, and tomorrow as well.

"We're caretakers of that legacy," Sims said. "And it's vital that we take good care of what we already have. But we can't stop here. We have to think about the future, too. Our civic grandfathers left us a wonderful gift—something that every resident of Spokane can enjoy. We need to do the same for our grandchildren."

RICK & SUSIE GRAETZ PHOTOS

Above: Designed by Kirtland Cutter and built in 1898, Patrick Clark's mansion is home to an award-winning restaurant today.

Right: Once one of the most elegant hotels in the West, the Davenport Hotel graces Spokane's historic downtown.

Facing page: Spokane's age of elegance comes alive as one tours the historic Campbell House designed by Kirtland Cutter.

Kirtland Cutter

Few individuals have left such a visible and lasting mark on the face of Spokane as Kirtland K. Cutter. Then again, few have been so doubly blessed with ability and opportunity as this bank-clerk-turned-architect.

Regarded by many as one of the finest architects ever to work in the Northwest, Cutter practiced in Spokane from 1889 until 1923. He worked in virtually every architectural style of the day, displaying always a keen eye for detail and a remarkable ability to successfully synthesize the many elements in his design repertoire. "He had what we call a soft pencil," said Ken Brooks, one of Spokane's most successful contemporary architects. "He had that wonderful flair for the decorative, yet he always saw the big picture. He tied it all together very neatly and usually did it on quite a grand scale."

Indeed, Cutter-designed buildings are among the most grandiose ever built in the region. The Davenport Hotel, the Spokane Club, and the Patrick Clark mansion—to name only a few of his works here—all survive today as impressive monuments to Cutter's talents. But at least some of the credit must go to Cutter's associates, particularly his partner, Carl Malmgren, and to his patrons, as well.

Cutter's artistic visions may never have been built without Malmgren's engineering expertise. And one must remember that he practiced in Spokane during a period of incredible social, cultural and economic growth. It was a time when fabulous fortunes were made seemingly overnight, and this new wealth was ostentatiously displayed in magnificent mansions. Often as not, it was Cutter to whom newly minted millionaires

Life at the turn-of-the-century, fine arts collections, regional history exhibits and Native American artifacts are on display in the Cheney Cowles Museum and the historic Campbell House.

turned for creations that would stand as monuments to their success and status.

One such millionaire was Patrick F. "Patsy" Clark, an Irish immigrant who made his fortune in the Coeur d'Alene mining country. He told Cutter to spare no effort or expense in building for him the most elegant home in the West. Around a spectacular eight-by-fourteen-foot stained-glass window, attributed by some architectural historians to Tiffany and possibly the first of the famed New York design studio's creations to be used in construction west of Chicago, Cutter produced a home of epic proportions. Built largely of materials and by craftsmen imported from Europe, the Clark mansion (which today houses Patsy Clark's restaurant, one of Spokane's finest) is one of the most exquisitely finished homes ever built in Washington. The twenty-six-room villa is built of specially made brick and trimmed with sculptured sepia sandstone from Italy. Inside, Cutter cleverly combined Roman, Egyptian, French and Moorish design influences. The large, Louis XIV-styled drawing room just off the entry foyer features hand-painted ceiling murals, gold-plated light fixtures and fireplace ornamentation, and two more Tiffany stained-glass windows. The original dining room, trimmed in gopher wood, has twenty-seven hand-carved monks' heads, each with a different facial expression, adorning the ceiling beam ends. The walls are covered with hand-woven Beauvais tapestry. Completed in 1898, three years after it was commissioned, the Clark mansion is said to have cost its owner $1 million.

"The quality of his work, of course, speaks for itself," said University of Washington architectural historian Meredith Clausen. "But you have to remember that he had the good fortune to work with a very wealthy clientele. In at least a few cases, Cutter was given carte blanche. He had opportunities other architects would have killed for."

Kirtland Kelsey Cutter, born in 1860 to a prominent Ohio banking family, arrived in Spokane Falls, Washington Territory, in 1886. He had attended the Art Students League in New York City and had studied painting, sculpture and design in the capitals of Europe, but he had never undertaken a formal study of architecture. A true sophisticate, the twenty-six-year-old bachelor came West with his books and his Bond Street wardrobe. Prematurely bald, Cutter also brought along his collection of wigs, each cut a little longer than the one before it, which for years he would wear in rotation to simulate growing hair. Unable to support himself as an artist, Cutter took work at the First National Bank, where his uncle, Horace Cutter, was cashier.

His architectural career was born from the ashes of the fire that devastated Spokane in the summer of 1889. During the construction boom that followed, Cutter and other Spokane architects were given the opportunity to rebuild the city literally from the ground up. Truly, he was a man who found himself in the right place at the right time with the right talents, and his career flourished.

Cutter emerged as much more than just a leading local architect. He designed Andrew Carnegie's summer retreat in the mountains of upstate New York; Kirtland Hall, a building named for his grandfather, Professor Jared P. Kirtland, on the campus of Yale; the mammoth log-and-stone Idaho State Pavilion at the 1893 Chicago World's Fair, and dozens of other buildings throughout the United States. Cutter received national awards for his residential work in Southern California, where he lived and worked from 1923, when he left Spokane, until his death in 1939 at the age of seventy-nine.

In 1921, *Architect & Engineer,* a leading trade periodical, visited Spokane and was impressed with the "rare architectural force and genius for design" in Cutter's work. By this time, however, the gilded age in the history of Spokane had begun to tarnish. The grand commissions to which Cutter had become accustomed were increasingly scarce. Beset with financial troubles, he left for California in the autumn of 1923.

A few days before he departed, Cutter sat down with a reporter for *The Spokesman-Review* to reflect on his years in Spokane. "Never have I completed a commission without wishing I could do it all over again and do it much better," he told the newspaperman. "Some of my first homes here…have been treated very kindly by the vines that cover their early faults. I always built to achieve the effect of age, at least to make the building fit its surroundings to look as if it had grown there and not been superimposed. I have been criticized for that quality many times, but when the wind and weather complete the work I started, the owners are usually reconciled to the idea."

RICK & SUSIE GRAETZ

ANNE C. WILLIAMS/THE SPOKESMAN-REVIEW

Above: Agriculture is an important part of Spokane's economy.

Right: Field work on the Palouse.

Facing page: Whitworth College situated on the far north side of Spokane, has a reputation for excellence in education.

Don Hamilton/Courtesy Whitworth College

A Place to Learn and Work

In its first 100 years, Spokane found its wealth in the land. The silver and lead mines of North Idaho, the wheat fields of the Palouse, the heavily timbered mountains to the north all contributed mightily to the building of the city. Railroads hauled ore, grain and lumber to distant markets and delivered automobiles, furniture, clothing, and a host of other goods here, establishing Spokane as the transportation and trade capital of a far-flung region.

In its second century, Spokane's economy has been reborn. The historic dependence on mining, agriculture and timber has given way to diversification that has fueled a boom in the 1990s and promises more economic growth in the years ahead. Spokane is now the largest medical center between Minneapolis and Seattle. Computer companies such as Hewlett-Packard are a dynamic presence. Kaiser Aluminum has upgraded its Spokane manufacturing plants, and Boeing has built a new production facility here. Six colleges and universities make Spokane an educational center today and also train the skilled work force and the business and community leaders of tomorrow.

"Some very fundamental changes have occurred and change is going to continue to occur," said Eastern Washington University economist Shik C. Young. "We're seeing more diversification…and in the long run that helps Spokane's economy greatly. It broadens the base and makes us less vulnerable" when economic winds suddenly shift, as they did in the 1980s. Those were rough years for Spokane. Natural resources industries went into a prolonged skid. Demand for timber products all but vanished, farm profits plummeted, and mines that had been running double shifts suddenly shut down. Spokane retailers felt the pain. Out-of-work loggers and miners don't buy many TVs or dining-room sets. Slowly, however, the tide turned; and as Spokane bounced back and even began to boom, it also started to bloom in new ways.

Consider the growth of higher education in Spokane. Washington State University has opened a Spokane branch campus. Eastern Washington University, which for years had offered a few classes here, has shifted whole programs into Spokane. Gonzaga University has made major investments both in its campus and in its academic programs. Whitworth College and Spokane's two community colleges joined WSU, EWU and Gonzaga in collaboration with government and local business and industry to launch the Spokane Intercollegiate Research and Technology Institute, anchor of the forty-eight–acre Riverpoint Higher Education Park that is developing at the eastern edge of downtown.

THE SPOKESMAN-REVIEW

Rivalry is intense between the Zags of Gonzaga and neighboring Eastern Washington University Eagles at the Martin Centre on the Gonzaga campus.

SIRTI was created to build sustainable economic growth for Spokane by involving academics, business and government in a partnership that will spark innovation in manufacturing, biotechnological, environmental and information-based industries.

"Our job basically is to help create and manage the new technology-based economy," said SIRTI spokeswoman Mary Joan Hahn. "We want to help innovative regional businesses get new products out of the lab and into the marketplace by giving them access to the expertise and resources of the academic and government partners."

Businesses with good ideas get access not only to SIRTI's network of experts, but also to its state-of-the-art facilities to research, test, develop, and market new products and processes. Washington Water Power is working with SIRTI in an effort to find a way to adapt fuel-cell technology now used to generate electricity in spacecraft to a system that would be practical in heating and lighting homes. A computers-in-business training program piloted by SIRTI is helping the 2,500 Spokane area firms that do business

Gonzaga University is a highly respected Jesuit school located near downtown along the Spokane River. DEREK HANSON/GONZAGA UNIVERSITY

with Fairchild Air Force Base get a jump on the mandate that all federal contractors begin submitting bids and invoices electronically by the year 2000.

Gonzaga sits directly across the Spokane River from the developing higher education park. The private Jesuit school, founded in 1887, is Spokane's oldest university. In 1995, Gonzaga was ranked by *U.S. News and World Report* as the third-best regional university in the West. Father Bernard J. Coughlin, who in 1996 became Gonzaga's chancellor after twenty-two years as its president, has long played an active role in Spokane's business community and has worked to make the university an increasingly vital part of life in Spokane. During his years at Gonzaga, Coughlin built a $50 million endowment fund, a $15 million scholarship fund and raised $8 million for professorships. He directed a $72 million campus capital improvement campaign that since 1984 has resulted in the construction of the Foley Library, the Jundt Art Center and Museum, the Martin Centre athletic facility, and new buildings for the schools of engineering, education and business administration.

"Gonzaga has been a distinguished resource in the intellectual, economic, social, artistic and political life of the community," Coughlin said. "But when all is said and done, the university is a good citizen primarily by doing what it does best and what it is uniquely qualified to do: provide excellent education, prepare leaders, and develop and train capable, responsible, moral citizens."

The health care industry also is growing here, and today Spokane is one of the largest medical centers in the West. It has six major hospitals and the two biggest, Sacred Heart Medical Center and Deaconess Medical Center, are the second- and third-largest in Washington. The size of the health care market served by Spokane is about the same as Seattle's. People come to Spokane from throughout the intermountain West to seek medical treatment.

Spokane has a national reputation for medical innovation and quality patient care. The Health Care Finance Administration recently ranked Sacred Heart, which has active heart, lung and renal transplant programs, the third-best medical center in the nation. Sacred Heart and Deaconess also have two of the best-equipped neonatal intensive care facilities in the region. Holy Family Hospital is well-regarded for its women's health center. The mission of the Heart Institute of Spokane, founded in 1989, is to reduce the impact of cardiovascular disease through cardiac-patient care, education, and research. It is the only freestanding heart catheterization facility in the Pacific Northwest. Spokane's medical community is active in research on a number of fronts. The Heart Institute is sponsoring a study of the benefits of aspirin and other drugs for relieving heart conditions. Doctors at Deaconess are conducting research on a new clot-busting drug that could help increase the flow of blood to the heart. All Spokane hospitals are involved in a joint study targeted at preventing adverse drug reactions in elderly patients.

As an industry, health care is the largest single sector of the local employment picture. There are about 1,000 physicians, 4,500 registered nurses, 400 pharmacists, 250 physical therapists, and 200 dentists in Spokane. Add in technicians and others in related medical jobs and about 19,000 people—roughly one out of every ten people working in Spokane—earn their livings in the health care field. And most earn very good livings. Local health care payrolls totaled more than $400 million in 1995.

Spokane has had success courting high-tech companies. Hewlett-Packard built a research and manufacturing facility at Liberty Lake in the Spokane Valley in 1979. It opened with forty-one employees. Since then, Hewlett-Packard's Spokane operation has outgrown its original plant, expanding into a 225,000-square-foot facility where 875 workers do research and make test equipment for the mobile phone industry. Hewlett-Packard also has acted as something of a magnet. Altech, Telect, Olivetti, Northern Technologies, Itron and Screentech all have built nearby, and in 1995 Egghead Software moved its corporate headquarters from Issaquah, Washington into the two buildings at Liberty Lake that Hewlett-Packard built back in 1979.

Farmland north of Spokane.

LARRY MAYER

    Many Spokane businesses have a strong environmental ethic. Mountain Gear owner Paul Fish hosts monthly Sierra Club meetings at his outdoor equipment store on North Division, and he and his employees regularly volunteer for trail or river cleanup work. And when important environmental legislation is on the docket in Congress, he allows anyone who wants to call back to Washington, D.C., to use his store's phone to voice their opinion. "They don't have to agree with me," Fish insists. "I'll still pay for the call." But it's a safe bet that most of Mountain Gear's patrons share Fish's outlook. "A clean and healthy environment is both our heritage and our future," he said.

    The local passion for all things outdoors has helped create a booming retail market here for all manner of recreation equipment, from Roller Blades to rock-climbing gear. Fish, who got started in the business by sewing custom backpacks in his living room, has built a good business—Mountain Gear consists of a growing mail-order trade, along with the 14,000-square foot Spokane store—by helping to build interest in non-motorized outdoor sports. "Everything we sell, we teach," Fish said. "We have classes in canoeing, kayaking, in-line skating, backpacking, you name it."

Simon Craven and Becky Tomlinson have made a business of catering to Spokane's taste for good coffee. Craven spent several years managing restaurants in California before going to work in 1991 for a young firm called Seattle's Best Coffee. There, he got on-the-job training in the science of roasting beans and the art of creating flavorful blends. He also got an insider's view of the exploding gourmet coffee market. Having learned the trade, he and Tomlinson went looking for a place to start their own coffee roastery. With research, they narrowed the list of possibilities to Atlanta, Minneapolis and Spokane, finally settling on Spokane, Craven said, "because we found a hidden sophistication here, a real appreciation of what we do, which is true specialty coffee."

A roaster of coffee for the wholesale market, Craven's Coffees opened in a small streetfront space in Carnegie Square in April of 1993. Business boomed almost immediately. "We had the great good fortune to show up in the right place with the right product at just the right time," Craven said. The company has created custom blends for several of Spokane's best restaurants, and also has gotten its coffees onto grocery store shelves around the Northwest.

COURTESY EASTERN WASHINGTON UNIVERSITY

Only fifteen miles from Spokane, Eastern Washington University is a short commute for students.

74

Rick & Susie Graetz

Above: The Heart Institute of Spokane is a diagnosis, rehab and research center for heart patients. Sacred Heart Medical Center ranked as the third-best medical center in the nation by the Health Care Finance Administration.

Right: Students find Whitworth College's wooded campus conducive to studying.

Alan Bisson/Courtesy Whitworth College

From Fort Wright to Fairchild

On September 10, 1941, Spokane civic and business leaders were notified that the U.S. War Department had selected the city as the site for a new regional Army Air Corps supply depot and maintenance base. There was just one catch: the government would have to get the land it wanted for the air depot at no cost.

It took the Spokane Area Chamber of Commerce less than a week to raise $121,133 to buy 2,400 acres of farm land on the West Plains. Every dime of that money was raised locally. Washington Water Power Company wrote the first check, for $10,000. Other Spokane businesses and business groups followed suit, together giving more than $100,000. The rest came as donations from individuals, in amounts big and small. Former Washington Gov. Clarence Martin gave $2,500. Charles d'Urbal, a French teacher at Lewis and Clark High School, gave $5. With war looming on the horizon, it was a grand showing of Spokane's patriotism. It also was an incredibly wise investment in the city's future.

That investment of $121,133 in 1941 has since returned many billions of dollars to the Spokane economy. Fairchild Air Force Base today is Spokane's largest single employer, with nearly 5,000 military personnel and civilian workers at

ALAN BISSON

Fairchild Air Force Base plays an important role in the economy and everyday life of Spokane.

the base. Fairchild's annual economic impact on the local economy, according to a 1995 Chamber of Commerce report, is $260 million.

"Fairchild is a huge, huge presence in Spokane," said C. Michael Archer, director of military affairs for the chamber. "I think most people are aware of the economic benefit of having the base here. It's hard to argue with 5,000 jobs. What a lot of people don't realize is that Spokane benefits in so many other ways. People from Fairchild invest tens of thousands of hours of volunteer time in our community. They're Big Brothers. They help build Habitat for Humanity houses. They work with the Boy Scouts, with local churches. Frankly, I'm always amazed that some 25-year-old airman will work so darn hard to make Spokane a better place, when it isn't even his hometown."

Fairchild is home to the 92nd Air Refueling Wing, with five squadrons of KC-135 stratotankers, the most at any military base in the world. It also is home to the oldest and largest U.S. Air Force survival school, where flight crew members learn skills needed to survive if their planes should go down behind enemy lines.

Fairchild's military role has changed in recent years, reflecting a larger change in the Air Force itself during the 1990s. Fairchild was historically a bomber base, and its huge, lumbering B-52s, which saw action in Korea and Vietnam, were familiar sights in the Spokane sky for many years until 1994. That year, the 92nd Bomb Wing was deactivated, its B-52s reassigned to other bases, and replaced at Fairchild by the 92nd Air Refueling Wing and its KC-135 tankers.

The Air Force established the Fairchild Survival School in 1966. About 4,700 people go through the seventeen-day Fairchild survival course each year. After classroom training at the base, survival students head for the nearby wilderness, where they get real-life lessons in building shelter, catching food, reading the stars for direction, and taking evasive action. "It's kind of like a very, very intense Boy Scout wilderness course," said Master Sergeant Dan Conrad. "It's tough, but you learn what you need to get you back home alive."

Nobody knows that better than Captain Scott O'Grady, the Spokane schoolboy-turned-fighter pilot who was shot down over Bosnia in 1995. After his dramatic rescue, O'Grady said it was his Fairchild Survival School training that enabled him to elude would-be captors for several days.

Spokane's military association predates the Air Force, and even its predecessor, the Army Air Corps. In fact, it predates even the Wright brothers' historic first flight by four years. In 1899, the U.S. Army built Fort Wright here, after residents requested protection from Indians. In 1922, Fort Wright became the headquarters for both the 58th Infantry and the 4th Infantry. In the 1930s, there were constant rumors that the fort would shut down as part of a nationwide military cutback. Nonetheless, it continued as the regional headquarters for Army training and ROTC programs. It was also a center for the Civilian Conservation Corps. In 1933, the fort housed 325 Army personnel and 1,500 CCC recruits. During the 1940s, Fort Wright served as a training site, and

Lake Coeur d'Alene's allure is a magnet to all, including Fairchild Air Force Base personnel.

as a hospital. Later, it was considered briefly as a site for the Air Force Academy, before being decommissioned in 1957.

Master Sergeant Conrad, a native of Washington, D.C., has been all around the world during his twenty-plus years in the Air Force. He requested his assignment to Fairchild. "Spokane is a very nice city in a very beautiful part of the world," he said. Conrad isn't the only airman who thinks that way. Fairchild ranks No. 2 as the domestic duty station most frequently requested by Air Force personnel, trailing only Hickam Air Force Base in Honolulu.

When he retires, Conrad said, Spokane is where he plans to stay. And again, he has plenty of company. In 1996, there were more than 7,600 people in and around Spokane collecting military pensions. "It's a great community that has always made military men and women, and their families, feel very welcome," Conrad said. "I guess a lot of us feel so welcome here we just decide to stay."

Rick & Susie Graetz

Above: Beautiful turn-of-the-century buildings house students at the Mukogawa Fort Wright Institute.
Facing page: Mukogawa students receive intensive instruction in English and American studies.

Education International-Style

When Mukogawa Women's University of Nishinomiya, Japan, opened its first foreign branch campus in Spokane in 1990, school officials likened the Mukogawa Fort Wright Institute here to a cultural bridge that would bring Japanese students to the United States for a first-hand view of American life. As many people have since learned, this bridge to cultural understanding can be traveled both ways.

During their semester of study in Spokane, all Mukogawa students are matched with local host families through the school's weekend homestay program. The home visits are intended to deepen the students' understanding of America by enabling them to participate in American family life. For Spokane host families, the happy return on this simple investment of hospitality is that they usually get just as much out of the experience as the Japanese students.

Ed and Kathy Springer and their children, Heidi and Adam, got involved with the host program early on and have had two dozen or more Mukogawa students as weekend guests. "Real cultural exchange happens on a person-to-person level," said Ed Springer, a cameraman for KHQ-TV. "Having the girls spend a few days in our home allows us to learn a lot about one another, about how we're different and how we're the same. We share our lives with them, but they share themselves and their culture with us."

Since the Mukogawa Fort Wright Institute opened in 1990, more than 1,200 Spokane

An authentic traditional tea room is part of the Mukogawa campus.

families have opened their homes to Mukogawa students. "It's supposed to be for just one weekend, but it rarely ends there," said Ed Tsutakawa, Mukogawa vice president. "During their semester in Spokane, many students are invited back three or four times, maybe more."

Host families are asked to allow the young Japanese women to see how Americans really live their day-to-day lives—and to let the students participate as much as possible. "They help prepare meals, load the dishwasher, play with the pets, you name it," Ed Springer said. "But we also try to spice it up with activities that they wouldn't get to do at home. They seem to love getting out into the country around Spokane, probably because they have so little open space in Japan. We might go out to Hayden Lake and take a hike or a boat ride."

Mukogawa Women's University, founded in 1939, is one of the oldest and largest women's educational institutions in Japan. Students who come to Spokane to attend the

Mukogawa Fort Wright Institute are typically eighteen- to twenty-year-old sophomore English majors enrolled in Mukogawa's junior college or its university program.

The Mukogawa Fort Wright Institute occupies a historic seventy-two-acre campus that was originally developed as a U.S. Army post. The handsome brick buildings, most of which date back to the early 1900s, were officers' quarters and barracks. Fort Wright was an active military site from 1899 until 1957, when it was declared surplus property and turned over to the city of Spokane. The site was subsequently sold to the Sisters of the Holy Names, who operated Fort Wright College, a small liberal arts institution, until 1982. The nuns sold the campus to the Japanese in 1990 for $3 million.

Mukogawa has invested heavily in the site. Major remodeling has been done to three classroom buildings, two office buildings, nine dormitories and two faculty houses. The student dining hall was enlarged to almost double its original size, and the campus grounds have been brightened by plantings of flowers and trees and the installation of turn-of-the-century–style street lamps.

Perhaps the most impressive addition to the campus is the new library and resource center completed in 1994. This $5 million facility—which houses a library and study area, classrooms, a computer center, offices and an authentic Japanese tea room—blends beautifully with the neo-Georgian red-brick structures built in 1906 when Fort Wright was a fledgling U.S. Army post. Visitors to campus often mistake the new structure for two nicely preserved old Army buildings that have been joined together at the midsection by a modern-looking, single-story sweep of glass. The tea room, built entirely without nails using special woods, stone and other natural materials, looks out onto a small garden from the main floor of the new resource center. Inside the twelve-foot-by-fifteen-foot room, Mukogawa students practice the ancient art of *chado,* the ceremonial serving of tea and small cakes. The traditional Japanese tea ceremony, a quiet ballet of respectful gestures and elegant pauses, is a reminder than both enterprise and contemplation are important aspects of life.

Such things as the tea ceremony provide important links to home for the young Japanese women attending the Fort Wright Institute. But while here Mukogawa students are purposefully immersed in American culture and the English language. In the classroom, they read, write and speak English. The institute's American studies program includes classes in U.S. history, politics, literature, film, poetry, pop culture and music. The students also are encouraged to use English in everyday conversation outside the classroom. They go shopping and sightseeing around Spokane. In winter, they take ski lessons. In spring, all Mukogawa students traditionally participate in Bloomsday.

"It's all part of them learning to understand us and us learning to understand them," said Ed Springer. "That understanding, the friendships that are formed, the connections that are made, will help all of us have a better future."

Rick & Susie Graetz

Above: Beautiful and challenging golf courses like The Creek at Qualchan abound in the Spokane Valley. Facing page: The Spokane Polo Club, traditional champions of the Northwest since 1915.

A Place to Play

For people who love the outdoors, the Spokane area just might be heaven's back yard. Want thrills? There's kayaking and rafting on wild, whitewater rapids, and black-diamond skiing. Something serene? Spokane has perhaps the country's finest collection of public golf courses, and miles and miles of trails for hiking and biking. And that's just what's available to folks who insist on hanging around town. Gas up the rig, strap your gear to the roof rack, hit the road and you can be in the middle of some serious fun in practically no time.

In July of 1995, *Outside* magazine profiled seven American cities in a cover story titled "Dream Towns." These, according to the magazine, are communities that at least raise "the possibility of perfect living in a perfect place." By *Outside*'s definition, that means mountains, water and wilderness, of course, but also good bookstores, a lively cultural scene, nice neighborhoods and a career opportunities. Sound like any place you know? It should. Spokane topped the writer's livability list.

Indeed, the great outdoors offers so many tantalizing possibilities to people who live around here that often the real challenge is choosing which type of activity to enjoy on any given day. Check the calendar. Spin the compass. There's some kind of fun waiting out there for just about everybody.

The Spokane River offers all sorts of water sports: swimming, fishing, canoeing, rafting, kayaking, water skiing, all within minutes of the city's heart. Nature watchers enjoy the greenery and the birds and other wildlife found along its banks. Bicyclists,

Mount Spokane is a favorite recreation destination winter or summer.

in-line skaters and others spin their wheels along the Centennial Trail.

The wildest form of get-wet fun takes place in the whitewater rapids just a couple of miles downstream from downtown. In spring and summer, members of the Spokane Canoe and Kayak Club and the Northwest Whitewater Association rendezvous at Riverside State Park, a skinny but lengthy 8,000-acre preserve just northwest of the city, to soak up some chilling after-work excitement in a stretch of river that roars through landmark rock formations. "The Spokane is really underestimated as a whitewater river," said Bart Rayniak, a member of both organizations. "You have Class IV drops at Bowl and Pitcher and Devil's Toenail." On Rayniak's personal fun meter, running rapids in a raft or a kayak measures "better than the best rollercoaster you've ever been on, and it's very safe as long as you know what you're doing and have the right gear." He recommends that anyone testing the river wear a helmet, a wet suit and, of course, a personal flotation vest.

People from Spokane love to play in North Idaho, home to some of the West's most beautiful big lakes. Coeur d'Alene, Pend Oreille and Priest, Idaho's three largest lakes, have miles of shoreline that provide summer cabin sites for thousands of Spokane residents. Thousands more keep boats on North Idaho's lakes or just enjoy a weekend at one of the many public campgrounds on the lakeshore.

"North Idaho is Spokane's playground," said Rick Just, Boise-based spokesman for the Idaho Department of Parks and Recreation. "For my money, Priest Lake is just about the most beautiful place in the whole world. I sure wish I could spend as much time there as people from Spokane." On any summer weekend, he said, about 40 percent of the people overnighting at one of the state campgrounds at Priest Lake, about two and a half hours north of the city, are from Spokane.

Pend Oreille is the biggest of the three big lakes. Its southernmost bay is only about an hour and a quarter from Spokane. Sailors like the big breezes that sweep down off the steep mountainsides around the lake. Fishermen like the big kamloops and kokanee that swim its cold, deep waters. The lakeside town of Sandpoint is home to a dozen or so art galleries, and to the Festival at Sandpoint, a two-week music festival that features classical, country, jazz and rock.

Of the three big lakes, Coeur d'Alene gets the heaviest use by Spokane residents, if for no reason other than its proximity

DAN PELLE/THE SPOKESMAN-REVIEW

Winter doesn't keep Spokane residents inside—here a local makes a ski trail out of snow-covered city streets.

to the city. Just thirty-five minutes east of downtown, this stunning blue jewel is wrapped by 135 miles of forested shoreline that curls around cozy bays and inlets. This has been the summertime favorite for generations of Spokane's lake-cabin owners. Today, it's also popular with "landless" lake residents—boaters who weekend on the lake, overnighting at one of the lake's many public docks, at a boat-access campground or just anchoring offshore in some quiet bay.

Golf is a summertime passion for thousands of Spokane residents. Lucky for them, the city has some of the best courses around. Each of Spokane's seven city- and county-owned golf courses has a unique character and identity, yet collectively they are all scenic, enjoyable to play for golfers of a wide range of abilities, and, perhaps most astonishing, extremely affordable.

Indian Canyon, a municipal course built in the 1930s, is something of a legend in the golfing world, and is an annual fixture on the *Golf Digest* list of the nation's top public courses. The Canyon is hilly and heavily wooded, a challenging course "designed to test second shots and [a golfer's] ability to handle every lie in the book, except the little white one," according to Harry Missildine, former sports editor of *The Spokesman-Review* and several times the winner of the Spokane Municipal Golf Championship.

There are fourteen public and private golf courses in Spokane County, and an equal number in Coeur d'Alene, Post Falls and other neighboring communities close enough to qualify as local. "There's no place in the country with the quality, the variety and the affordable prices you find at golf courses in Spokane and North Idaho," said Bob Hamilton, a self-described "golf nut" who is the director of marketing at Schweitzer Mountain Resort, the Sandpoint ski area.

The truth is, the same can be said for the Spokane and North Idaho area's ski resorts. It would be tough to find another place that could match this area's collection of ski quality, variety and cost (regular prices for an adult all-day lift ticket in 1996 ranged from $15 to $35). Schweitzer and Kellogg's Silver Mountain are at the high end of the local scale in both quality and price. Schweitzer, which in the past decade has begun to emerge as a regional destination resort, is the bigger and arguably the better of the two resorts. Want to ski open bowls? Steep mogul fields? Narrow chutes? Cornices? Intermediate cruiser runs? Easy, groomed-within-an-inch-of-its-life beginner stuff? You'll find it all at both places. It's just that Schweitzer has more—2,350 skiable acres to 1,500 at Silver. It also has an on-the-mountain ski village, and artsy Sandpoint, with its restaurants, galleries and shops, has it hands-down over blue-collar Kellogg as a resort town. On a typical Saturday or Sunday, about half of the skiers at both resorts will have come from Spokane.

Mount Spokane, the 5,800-foot landmark just northeast of the city, 49 Degrees North at Chewelah, and Lookout Pass ski area just off Interstate 90 on the Idaho-Montana border, are smaller, less expensive skiing alternatives.

Winter isn't the only time Spokane residents get out and enjoy the area's mountains

RICK & SUSIE GRAETZ

Saturday afternoon at the park.

Rick & Susie Graetz Photos

Above: The view of the city from Indian Canyon Golf Course makes it difficult to keep your mind on the game.

Left: Best friends.

Rock climbers on the Minnehaha Rocks.

RICK & SUSIE GRAETZ

and hills. Mount Spokane State Park, site of the alpine ski resort and a popular network of well-maintained trails for cross-country skiers and snowmobilers, has no real off-season. It also attracts hikers, horseback riders, berry pickers and mountain bikers by the thousands.

The 13,821-acre high-country park, which is home to deer, bear, moose, cougar and just about every species of tree found in the Northwest, is also a favorite place for simply enjoying the region's wonderful flora and fauna. In 1995, state parks officials estimate, Mount Spokane had 860,000 visitors. Hikers, bird-watchers and other lovers of nature's quiet beauty also enjoy the Little Spokane River Natural Area north of the city, and the Dishman Hills Natural Area, which separates the suburban south Spokane Valley from the city's urban East Side. Both offer trails in a close-in natural setting, and

RICK & SUSIE GRAETZ

High school artists decorating the concrete pillars under the interstate highway.

the Little Spokane's lush woods support a large deer population, and a great blue heron rookery thrives in its marshes.

No organization has done more for outdoor recreation in the area than the Spokane Mountaineers. Founded in 1915 as the Spokane Walking Club, the organization offers comprehensive courses in mountaineering, backpacking and technical climbing, and has supported a wide variety of conservation and environmental causes. After completing Mountaineers' courses, students can participate in evening climbs at Minnehaha Rocks, or in ascents of mountain peaks around the region. Several climbers who got their starts with the Mountaineers have scaled the tallest mountains in the world, including Everest.

ALAN BISSON

Basketball and sneakers take over the streets in June. Hoopfest is the largest 3-on-3 basketball tournament in the United States.

ALAN BISSON

Rick & Susie Graetz

Above: Biking with grandpa.

Left: Coeur d'Alene is a favorite get-away for Spokane golfers and water enthusiasts.

93

Sandra Bancroft-Billings/The Spokesman-Review

Above: Bloomies overflow the course at the ever-popular Bloomsday run.

Facing page: Artist David Govedare's sculpture "The Joy of Running Together" honors the Bloomsday race.

Bloomsday

Spokane is a place where one person can make a difference. Consider the case of a local long-distance runner named Don Kardong.

Back in 1977, a year after he had finished fourth in the marathon at the Montreal Olympics, Kardong organized a little fun run through the streets of Spokane. Fun run? In those days, most sensible folks considered the term to be an oxymoron. But Spokane was an early beachhead for the national fitness craze and 1,200 people turned out to take part in that first Bloomsday race—a truly amazing number, Kardong thought. Five thousand people ran the next year. In 1981, there were 15,000, and three years later, 30,000. Today, Bloomsday attracts more than 60,000 participants—ranging from world-class athletes racing for $100,000 in prize money, to local fitness buffs who want only a Bloomsday T-shirt and bragging rights when their names appear in the next day's newspaper, to senior citizens who simply enjoy a springtime stroll along the scenic 12-kilometer course with their grandkids.

"I'm still a little in awe of the way the whole thing has taken off," Kardong said. "I thought we had a lot of people that first year when 1,200 showed up to run. At that time, it would have been incomprehensible to me that Bloomsday would one day have 60,000-plus participants."

Bloomsday, which takes place in Spokane each year on the first Sunday in May, is the second-largest foot race in America and the biggest in which the time and place of every finisher is recorded. But Bloomsday is much more to Spokane than just a mad dash through the city's streets. It has flowered fully into a rite of spring, a celebration of good health and personal fitness, an exercise in community pride.

"It's my favorite day of the year in Spokane," said Kevin Gilmore. A runner whose aim each year is to better his personal Bloomsday record of fifty-one minutes, Gilmore is also co-owner, with chef Gina Lanza, of the Anaconda Grille, a wonderful Italian restaurant that is a favorite place for carbo loading on Bloomsday eve. "It's spring, the flowers are blooming, and the city looks absolutely gorgeous," he said. "Everybody is feeling good about Spokane. They're feeling good about themselves, about being alive. The city just glows."

The events a city chooses to embrace as its own reveal something of the character of that city. What does Bloomsday say about Spokane? It says that a great many people here pursue physical fitness as a way of life. It says that people here would much rather do than watch, that they like to be active participants in the life of their community. Perhaps most important, it says that Spokane knows how to pull together for something whose whole seems far greater than the sum of all its parts.

In barely twenty years, Bloomsday has become a part of the rhythm of life in Spokane. Like robins and buttercups, the first Bloomies-in-training are a clearly recognizable sign that spring is upon us, or nearly so. It's time for a winter-weary community to end the hibernation, to get outside and fill those lungs with fresh air, move those muscles, get that blood stirring again. As Spokane thaws, you'll see them out and about, alone, in twos and threes, sometimes in larger groups, puffing along the Centennial Trail, legging it up the South Hill, loping along Summit Boulevard.

An event like Bloomsday would not attract such phenomenal numbers of participants if Spokane had not embraced the fitness movement with the incredible enthusiasm exhibited here. At the same time, Bloomsday itself both stimulates and rewards that enthusiasm. And it spills over, generating interest in other healthful activities such as walking, cross-country skiing, swimming and bicycling. "The city's enthusiasm for fitness and Bloomsday feed off each other," Kardong said. "People decide they're going to participate in Bloomsday and they spend three or four months getting ready. They jog and ride their bikes and they start watching what they eat a little more carefully. Pretty soon, they work themselves into pretty good shape. They feel better physically and that makes them feel better about themselves emotionally. It's something they don't want to give up."

As Bloomsday has grown, it has also made room for those who are more flabby than fit, more flat-footed than fleet, more interested in having fun with friends and family than with burning up the race course. That first Bloomsday, the average finisher's time was just under an hour. Now, it takes the typical Bloomie a little more than two hours to reach the finish line. On the twentieth running of Bloomsday, it took one woman, Cecelia Kelly of Cheney, three hours and nineteen minutes to cover the course. She rode most of the way in a wheelchair pushed by relatives, but the 105-year-old woman walked across the finish line, gripping a cane in each hand. Tracy Walters, the finish-line public address announcer, crowed: "That's the spirit of Bloomsday, right there in that 105-year-old woman!"

Circulate among the crowd awaiting the start of the race and you'll see humanity in all its wonderful forms: Thick and thin, long and short, paunchy and powerful. Some are outfitted in high-tech running gear, some wear cut-off jeans and high-top Chuck Taylor All-Stars. A few look like they're headed for a Halloween party. (Is that Elvis over there standing next to the guy in the bride-of-Frankenstein costume?) The serious athletes are stretching, jogging, loosening up. Wander a little deeper into the crowd and you find people talking and laughing, singing, sipping coffee, snacking, mugging for photos. You'll catch one or two smoking. Many things motivate these people, but all share one goal: The finish line.

The downtown stampede starts when the starter's gun cracks at nine o'clock sharp, sending the elite runners on their way. Those greyhounds will be nearing the race's halfway point by the time the parents pushing baby strollers and others in the back of the pack even cross the official starting line. Three long streams flow along Main, Riverside and Sprague avenues, then merge west of downtown. The course contains two significant hills: Tombstone, a long gradual climb that takes runners past two cemeteries, and Doomsday, a shorter but steeper incline that is everything its name implies. At the top of Doomsday Hill, a twelve-foot vulture strikes a menacing pose. For those who escape the vulture's talons, the rest of the course is a flat, relatively easy two-mile romp back toward downtown, to the finish line at City Hall. There, runners, walkers and stragglers alike are greeted by cheers, the ever-blaring theme from "Rocky," and sculptor David Govedare's popular tribute to Bloomsday, "The Joy of Running Together," a collection of steel runners forever rounding the turn from Post Street onto Spokane Falls Boulevard.

It takes a lot of work to make Bloomsday work so well for so many. More than 5,000 volunteers help ensure that the whole affair comes off smoothly each year. They process registration forms for weeks ahead of time, man the water and first-aid stations along the race route, and hand those coveted T-shirts to each and every finisher afterward.

For all who participate, Bloomsday is an achievement. "For the individual who takes part, there's that glow of pride in accomplishing something," Don Kardong said. "For the community, it's the same thing. Spokane sees itself as a healthy city—a place where we can make good things happen."

ALAN BISSON

Left: Riverfront Park and downtown Spokane shine in the late afternoon sun.

Below: The twin spires of Our Lady of Lourdes Cathedral rise above downtown.

RICK & SUSIE GRAETZ

Rick & Susie Graetz

Rick & Susie Graetz

Above: More than 1,500 rose bushes blossom on Rose Hill in Manito Park.

Top: Brick beauties line Washington Street.

Right: Crops decorate nature's designs near Steptoe Butte.

Rick & Susie Graetz

From Broadway to Beethoven to big names, the Spokane Opera House has it all.

ALAN BISSON PHOTOS

Above: Excitement and entertainment at the Spokane Interstate Fair.

Left: The Lilac Festival is a spring tradition dating back to 1938.

103

Index

Italics indicate photographs

Abell, John 21, 45, 54
Adolfae, Mike 53
Agriculture *68*
Altech 72
Anaconda Grille 96
Apple, Bob 52
Archer, C. Michael 18, 78
Architecture 21–28
Balazs, Harold 16
Beck, Gary 16
Best of Broadway 10
Biking 85, 86
Bloomsday *94*, 95–97
Boeing 34, 69
Bookstores 85
Boulder Beach 42
Brooks, Ken 65
Burlington Northern Railroad 52
Busch, Ralph 16
Campbell House *65*
Canada Island *36*
Cannon Hill 50
Canoeing 85
Carnegie Square 47, 54, 74
Castle, The *2*
Cathedral of Saint John the Evangelist *23*
Centennial Trail *24*, 42, *44*, 86
Chamber of Commerce Building 28
Cheney Cowles Museum 15, *66*
City Ramp Garage 27
Clark, Patrick F. "Patsy" 66
Clausen, Meredith 67
Cliff Drive *20*
Cliff Park 48, 50
Clocktower 63
Coeur d'Alene *93*
Coeur d'Alene Park *60*
Comet Tavern 52
Community colleges 70
Comstock Park *58*
Conrad, Dan, Master Sgt. 78, 79
Copenhaver, Deborah 16
Craven, Simon 74
Craven's Coffees 74
Cutter, Kirtland 27, 28, 65–67
Davenport Hotel 28, *64*, 65
Davenport, Louis 28
Deaconess Medical Center 72
Dishman Hills Natural Area 91
Duncan Garden *51*, 62
Eastern Washington University 70
Education 70
Egghead Software 72
Esmeralda Golf Course *20*
Expo 74 16, 63
Fairchild Air Force Base 71, 76–79, *77*
Fairchild Survival School 78
Festival at Sandpoint 87
Fish, Paul 73–74
Fishing 85
Fitzgerald, Tonie 33
Fix, Penn 28

Fleury, Jacque Ferrell 34
Foley Library 71
Fort Wright 78
49 Degrees North ski area 88
G&B Select-A-Seat 10
Gaiser Conservatory 62
Gallinger, Holly 57
Gardening 31
Garland *23*, 47, 53
Garland Theater 53, *56*
Gilmore, Kevin 96
Goetzinger, Rolf 53
Golf 31, 85, 87–88
Gondola Skyride *41*
Gonzaga law school 21
Gonzaga University 16, *19*, 21, 34, 37, *39*, 70, *71*, 71–72
Gonzaga University crew *26*
Goodsell, Ethyl 33
Govedare, David 16, *95*, 97
Hahn, Mary Joan 70
Hamilton, Bob 88
Heart Institute of Spokane 72, 75
Hewlett-Packard 34, 72
Hiking 85
Hill, James J. 52
Hillyard *35*, *46*, 47, 52–53, 57
Hillyard Festival 52
Hillyard Laundry and Dry Cleaners 53
Holy Family Hospital 72
Hoopfest 91
Hoover, Frank 21
Indian Canyon golf course 88, *89*
Inland Empire Paper Company 42
Integrus Architecture 54
Itron 72
Jundt Art Center and Museum 16, 71
Kaiser Aluminum 69
Kardong, Don 95, 96, 97
Kayaking 85
Kellogg, Idaho 88
Kerr, Frank 53, 57
Kienholz, Edward 13–16
Lake Coeur d'Alene *8*, 18, *39*, 87
Lake Pend Oreille 15, *29*, 87
Lanza, Gina 96
Liberty Park *9*, *46*
Lilac City 33
Lilac Festival *103*
Little Spokane River 29
Little Spokane River Natural Area 91
Looff Carousel *59*, 63
Lower Spokane Indians 29
Lucas, Jack 10
Malmgren, Carl 65
Manito Park 45, 59, 62, *100*
Market Place 55
Martin Centre 71
Medical facilities *12*, 55, 69, 72
Metropolitan Performing Arts Center 8, *30*
Middle Spokane Indians 29
Millwood 42
Minnehaha Rocks *90*, 91
Missildine, Harry 88
Monroe Street Bridge *5*
Mount Spokane *20*, *86*

Mount Spokane ski resort 88
Mount Spokane State Park 90–91
Mountain Gear 73–74
Mukogawa Fort Wright Institute 80, 81–83, *82*
Mukogawa Women's University 81, 82
Natatorium Park 24
Native Americans 29
Nishinomiya, Japan *35*, 81
Nishinomiya Japanese Garden 62
North Coast Life Insurance 28
North Side 48
Northern Technologies 72
Northwest Fur Company 29
Northwest Whitewater Association 86
O'Grady, Scott, Capt. 78
Olivetti 72
Olmsted Brothers 48
Our Lady of Lourdes Cathedral *99*
Palouse 68
Parks *1*, *2*, *18*, 59, 88
Patrick Clark mansion *64*, 65
Patsy Clark's restaurant 66
Paulsen, August 24
Paulsen Center 24
Paulsen Medical and Dental Building 24
Pleasant Prairie rural school *25*
Pollution 38–39
Population 8
Priest Lake 87
Quinlivan, Judy 34, 61
Quinn, Tom 53
Rafting 85
Rayniak, Bart 86
Review Building 28
Riverfront Park *1*, 16, *36*, 37, 42, 59, 63, *98*
Riverfront Park Pavilion 63
Riverfront Park Petting Zoo *38*
Riverpoint Higher Education Park 70
Riverside State Park *25*, 86
Rockwood 50
Rose Hill 62, *100*
Sacred Heart Medical Center 72, 75
Salish Indians 29
Sandpoint, Idaho 87
Schneider, Franz 37
Schweitzer Mountain Resort 88
Screentech 72
Shioski, Roy 53
Silver Mountain ski resort 88
Sims, Ron 63
Ski resorts 31, 88–90
Skid Road 54
Skiing 85
Skywalks *12*
Smith, Marilyn 33
Soltero, Ray 38
South Hill *20*, 45, 47, 48, 50, 57, 62
Spiering, Ken 16, *58*
Spokane Area Chamber of Commerce 18, 76
Spokane Arena 10
Spokane Canoe and Kayak Club 86

Spokane Chiefs *11*
Spokane Club 28, 65
Spokane County Courthouse *7*
Spokane Falls *41*
Spokane Falls Community College *9*
Spokane Floral Association 33
Spokane House 29
Spokane Indians *33*, 37
Spokane Indians baseball team 50
Spokane Intercollegiate Research and Technology In 70–71
Spokane Interplayers Ensembl 34
Spokane Interplayers Ensemble 11
Spokane Interstate Fair *103*
Spokane Mountaineers 91
Spokane Opera House 8, 10, *102*
Spokane Park Board 48, 63
Spokane Polo Club 85
Spokane River *5*, *8*, 16, *25*, *26*, 29, *36*, 37–43, *40*, 63, 85
Spokane Symphony Orchestra 13
Spokane Valley 42, 47, 54
Springer, Ed 81, 83
Steptoe Butte *101*
Sullivan Park 42
Sumner Avenue *47*, 48
Swimming 85
Telect 72
The Creek at Qualchan golf course *84*
The Spokesman-Review 28, *32*, 67, 88
Thomas, Larry 53
Thompson, David 29
Tomlinson, Becky 74
Tour des Lacs *7*
Tsutakawa, Ed 82
U.S. Bank Building 24
United Way of Spokane 34
Upper Spokane Indians 29
Upriver Dam 42
Uptown Opera 8
Walters, Tracy 97
Washington State University 24, 33, 45, 70
Washington Street *100*
Washington Water Power 34, 70, 76
Water skiing 85
Weather 30–31
Weitz, Sue 21
Welch, Bob 11, 34
Welch, Joan 11
Wells, Julie 54
Wells, Ron 54
West Central 47, 50, 59
White, Aubrey L. 50, 61, 63
Whitworth College 69, 70, 75
Young, Shik C. 69

Michael Schmeltzer, a resident of Spokane for more than twenty years, has been a reporter and editor at *The Spokesman-Review* since 1980. He started his career as a journalist with the *Juneau* (Alaska) *Empire* in 1975, a year after graduating from Spokane's Rogers High School.